Praise for *My Teenage Zombie*

My Teenage Zombie is an essential to
zombie teen scare you. Pick up this l
zombie within. You just might find t

FAMILY THERAPIST AND FOUNDER OF THE LIFEOLOGY INSTITUTE

Parents will find inspiration from the wisdom, humor, and practical strategies in *My Teenage Zombie*. This book is filled with real-world examples that parents will be able to apply starting day one. In my thirty years working with parents and adolescents I have found it rare for a book to so effectively translate the complex struggles and emotions of modern teens into tools that parents can understand and use. David's hands-on approach to offering immediate solutions for parents struggling to support their teens will speak directly to both parents and professionals. Our practice will be offering this resource to all of our clients.

—SCOTT D. CANTER
MANAGING PARTNER, ACADEMIC ANSWERS DFW

As a former "teenage zombie" struggling with eating disorder, substance use, and self-esteem issues, I wish my parents had this book available to them. A must-read for all parents.

—BRIAN CUBAN
ATTORNEY AND AUTHOR OF *SHATTERED IMAGE: MY TRIUMPH OVER BODY DSYMORPHIC DISORDER*

My Teenage Zombie should be required reading for all parents trying to raise healthy teens! It offers hope for those who may think their family situation is too far gone and will help parents better understand and help their children navigate the tumultuous teenage years to successfully enter society with confidence and vision.

—BECKY VANCE
PRESIDENT & CEO, DRUG PREVENTION RESOURCES

Dr. Henderson has hit a home run with his latest book about a very important, yet frequently overlooked topic for all parents raising teenagers in these tumultuous times. Relevant, clearly written, and engaging, *My Teenage Zombie* is a must-read for everyone interacting with today's teenagers, in order to help them successfully evolve into the leaders of the next generation of our society. Most importantly, since his recommendations and guidance are centered on evidenced-based principles, parents can trust that Dr. Henderson's book can make a real difference in how they help their teenager grow into a healthy, emotionally-mature, and successful adult.

—Dr. Harold Urschel III
Board-Certified Addiction Psychiatrist,
Co-Founder of Enterhealth, and *New York Times*
Bestselling Author of *Healing the Addicted Brain*

As parents we often joke that children don't come with an instruction manual. Finally, we have one. Dr. Henderson does a masterful job of laying out a blueprint for parents that is rich in practical tools and strategies gleaned from years of experience as a psychiatrist working with adolescents and families. This book teaches parents not only how to navigate those tumultuous teenage years, but also how to build a foundation in the early years of life that will pave the way for stronger relationships and better equip them with a lifelong sense of motivation, direction, and determination. I would put this book at the top of every parent's reading list.

—Vanita Halliburton
President, Grant Halliburton Foundation

Converting our precious babies into confident, contributing members of society is daunting at best, and sometimes downright terrifying. As a recurring guest on *Mornings with Jeff & Rebecca*, Dr. Henderson has been a wealth of wisdom and resources for us personally, and for hundreds of thousands of our listeners. You will be better equipped because of this book!

—Rebecca Ashbrook Carrell and Jeff Taylor
Morning Show Hosts on 90.9 KCBI, Dallas–Ft. Worth

My Teenage Zombie

Resurrecting the Undead
Adolescent in Your Home

David L. Henderson, MD

W PUBLISHING GROUP

AN IMPRINT OF THOMAS NELSON

Published in Nashville, Tennessee, by W Publishing Group, an imprint
of Thomas Nelson. W Publishing and Thomas Nelson are registered
trademarks of HarperCollins Christian Publishing, Inc.

Thomas Nelson titles may be purchased in bulk for educational, business,
fund-raising, or sales promotional use. For information, please e-mail
SpecialMarkets@ThomasNelson.com.

Scripture quotations are taken from the Holy Bible, New International
Version®, NIV®. Copyright © 1973, 1978, 1984, 2011 by Biblica, Inc.™
Used by permission of Zondervan. All rights reserved worldwide. www.
zondervan.com. The "NIV" and "New International Version" are
trademarks registered in the United States Patent and Trademark Office by
Biblica, Inc.™

Library of Congress Control Number: 2016945747

ISBN 978-0-7180-3124-4

Printed in the United States of America

16 17 18 19 RRD 5 4 3 2

CONTENTS

CONTENTS

INTRODUCTION

The Rise of the Undead

D o you believe in zombies? I sure didn't. But then I encountered something in my clinical practice unlike anything I had ever seen before. It was early in my career as a physician, and I was working in a psychiatric emergency room in downtown Dallas. A nineteen-year-old man was escorted (I use that term loosely) into the building by five police officers, all burly men who could barely control the 170-pound mass of writhing, screaming, intoxicated fury who had once been an above average, courteous, and ambitious college student at the local state university.

Mesmerized by the scene before me, I only faintly heard the call from the nurse assigned to him. "Uh, Dr. Henderson, can I get a verbal order here, please?" She wasn't asking.

"Any allergies or other medical problems that we know of?" I asked.

"Nothing that we know of at this point," she replied.

"Okay, let's do a 10–2–50 IM, please." It was an order for one of the most powerful sedative combinations we use in psychiatry: 10 mg of Haldol, 2 mg of Ativan, and 50 mg of Benadryl, all

given intramuscularly while the patient is restrained, held pros-
trate on the floor. I'd seen staff members get seriously injured
during an intervention like this, so it was absolutely crucial that
everyone involved know their role exactly. As much as possible,
the patient's safety was our first priority, but we were also acutely
aware of the need for forceful restraint, due to how much danger
he posed to himself and others. Once the medication started to
take effect, we released the young man and quickly exited the
room, locking the door behind us.

Within seconds he was on his feet again, pacing the room,
eying me through the small Plexiglas window in the door that
separated us. He growled, pounded his fist against the door,
shouted a stream of unintelligible threats, and then went silent
for a brief moment, long enough for the two of us to observe
each other.

In that moment of unsettling tranquility, I felt a rush of fear
and sadness. Fear of my own fragility as a human reflected back
upon me by this suffering individual who was someone's son,
brother, boyfriend, classmate. But also sadness at the thought
of how quickly life can take an unexpected turn for the worse.
The young man before me—we later discovered his name was
Brian—never intended to end up in a hospital, let alone a psychiatric ward. Most likely, he had planned a fun evening with
his friends to escape the stress of a tough semester. Along the
way, however, something went seriously wrong.

Toxicology reports showed that Brian had ingested several
drugs, including ecstasy, alcohol, cocaine, and phencyclidine
(PCP) while at a fraternity party. These mind-altering chemicals swept through his brain like a flash flood, tearing down any
dams of self-restraint he possessed, leaving no barriers between

his feelings and his actions. In neuropsychological terms, we would say that Brian had lost his ability to make executive decisions. His actions were based purely on impulse without reasoning, planning, or self-reflection.

During the next forty-eight hours, the flood of chemicals that had rushed through Brian's system receded and his senses returned, including his sense of dignity and shame. He apologized profusely to staff and fellow patients alike when he realized all that had transpired during his mental "absence." His embarrassment was palpable. Though we all tried to make him feel at ease, let's face it: this was an experience we hoped he would never forget.

Unfortunately, Brian did forget. Several times during my tenure at the hospital, Brian returned in almost the exact same manner, always leaving with an apology but failing to follow through with the recommendations we made for him to avoid future hospitalizations. It was apparent that Brian's struggle with drugs and alcohol stemmed from a deeper struggle inside himself.

Brian had become a teenage zombie.

PART 1
Understanding the Attack

CHAPTER 1

The Teenage Zombie Defined

In the world of fiction, the undead are the most terrifying monsters I can imagine.

They are animated corpses that were once human, died, and by some supernatural means returned to an existence just short of life. They are tormented beings with an unquenchable drive to regain some semblance of what they once knew, and they pursue and consume their human counterparts in horrific ways. One might say that the undead have an insatiable lust for life but can only take it from others, never securing it for themselves.

As a metaphor, the undead represent adolescents and emerging adults whose psychological and social development have died. Erik Erikson, who proposed that the main task of adolescence is forming a healthy self-identity, would say that these young people are confused as to their purpose in life and their role in relationships.[1] They lack maturity, motivation, and purpose, exhibiting a helplessness and fear of responsibility. As a result, they seem destined to remain under their parents' care forever, consuming all their time, energy, and resources, just like a zombie would.

When considering the challenges of raising an adolescent, many parents feel the same childlike fear that audience members do when watching a zombie movie. The horrors we imagine might befall our kids and the very real possibility that we could be mentally and emotionally consumed by their struggles can lead us to the point of desperation. Many parents admit that they do not have the resources necessary to deal with these challenges.

At this time during your adolescent's development, he may feel torn between yearning for freedom and fear of surviving in the outside world. Meanwhile, you as a parent may feel helpless to love, support, guide, and empower him to thrive in, not just survive, this life.

In fact, many parents with teenagers are themselves facing a midlife crisis. They are internally battling the same issues they see playing out before them in the lives of their children: apathy; lack of direction; unwanted physical changes of aging; rebellious questioning of authority; experimentation with drugs, alcohol, and sexual expression; and resentful dependence on a constraining society. Is it really possible to escape this "undead" state of being?

The truth is that some of our worries may be unfounded, and there are effective remedies for most of the others. Once we understand how the characteristics of the zombies on screen parallel the struggles within our own children, we can start living like survivors, not victims, of our children's adolescence. Using themes and metaphors depicted in stories of the undead, I'm writing this book to help provide a clear framework by which you can practically and successfully help your teenager navigate an ever-lengthening stage of adolescence and successfully enter society with confidence and vision. It may even challenge us adults to consider where we are struggling with the circumstances of our own lives so that we may experience a freshness to life that we did not think possible before.

Have the Undead Invaded Your Home?

How do you know if you have an undead adolescent in your home? After all, the stage of adolescence is, in general, a challenging time for children and parents alike, even if it does progress with relatively few halting crises. When you consider the physiological changes within the body, the psychological challenges of forming a healthy identity, the difficulty of navigating platonic and romantic peer relationships, the desire to secure independence from the family of origin, and the burden of adopting ever-increasing responsibilities within society, you can see all the forces that contribute to making adolescence a stressful time. Many teens manage to grope their way through the fog and confusion of this stage of development unaffected by the undead all around them. Sometimes it can be hard to tell the living from the dead. So how do you know if your son or daughter is one of the infected?

A teenage zombie lacks the following three elements that are absolutely necessary to sustain life: spark, pulse, and fiber.

A Life Without Spark

We all know that the human brain is an electrical organ as much as it is a chemical one. Signals are transmitted throughout the body by nerves that send electrical signals to and from the brain.

Fictional zombies have brains that have been infected, usually by the bite of another zombie, and are therefore damaged. Their electrical system has gone haywire, and as a result, they act impulsively, without thinking. In other words, they lack the *spark* necessary for purposeful actions.

In zombie teenagers, the spark of their lives that is missing represents their *motivation*: that thing that drives them forward from day to day. Undead adolescents, at first glance, appear to lack this spark. They look comfortable with the circumstances of their lives and have little motivation for improvement. They may spend hours on the couch playing video games, watching television, reading blogs, or hanging out with friends. They may have few extracurricular activities or hobbies and spend most of their time at home. If they do have jobs, they have no desire for advancement and do the bare minimum of what is asked of them by their bosses. In school they scrape by with Cs earned at the last minute by turning in makeup work and cramming for exams. Their teachers consistently say, "They just don't apply themselves." Procrastination, tardiness, forgetfulness, and lack of initiative are common. Instead of these teenagers pulling their own weight at home, their parents feel like they are dragging their children's dead corpses everywhere they go.

The spark-less zombie living in your home is in one of two states of being—meaninglessness or mindlessness.

Meaningless Zombies

Kids who are living as meaningless zombies are like the slow, aimlessly meandering zombies of 1960s and 1970s horror films. They look at life through a lens of cynicism, discouragement, and purposelessness.

The key feature born out of the meaninglessness these zombies experience is a lack of motivation. The activities they want to participate in are limited significantly. Perhaps they lie in bed all day, barely eating, isolating themselves from family and friends. They might have difficulty concentrating on the tasks before them, resulting in failing grades, unfinished chores, and poor self-care. Physically, their energy is low. They are lethargic and difficult to inspire. Zombies like these are scary because of the hopelessness and lifelessness they exude. Parents fear that their children's inaction will end in a life that has irreversibly passed by them.

For some, it may move beyond the normal phase of adolescent brooding toward a more serious clinical depression. One of the features of depression is *anhedonia*—an internal loss of happiness in the midst of normally pleasurable experiences.[2] This apathy for life taints everything they do—or more accurately, everything they *don't* do. It is important to consider this when working with your child. He or she might not be lazy, undisciplined, or defiant, but rather discouraged, depressed, or defeated in some aspect of his life. If this is the case, you should seriously consider professional intervention.

Mindless Zombies

The mindless zombie is like the crazed, super-fast zombies of modern horror flicks. Think *World War Z*. These zombies don't focus on the meaninglessness of life. In fact, they don't appear to focus at all. These zombies usually rush into life like a freight train that has jumped the tracks. They seem to lack the conscious awareness necessary to have or understand the motivation behind their behaviors.

We might say that these kids are impulsive, absentminded, rash, or even foolhardy. Many have been diagnosed with attention-deficit/hyperactivity disorder (ADHD). They are often swayed by intense emotions, subjective sensing, and intuition. Rational thought is a slow second to the more overwhelming emotional surges of the moment. Their higher, more logical brain functions only kick in after the fact, mainly in an effort to explain their behaviors, which they do not fully understand. Unfortunately, because of this, they may be labeled as dishonest or manipulative. When parents consider their child's actions, they are often left asking, "What were you thinking?" The usual response from the child is, "It seemed right at the time!"

Parents fear this kind of zombie because of the potential irreparability of their quick, poorly planned actions. Instead of life passing by them, life seems to move too slowly for them. They rush on ahead with every opportunity, demonstrating an unconscious, unmediated pursuit of pleasure. It is not that they don't care about you or others. They just don't think to care. The intensity of their drive leaves them unable to think or consider any higher purpose beyond their immediate self-gratification.

A Life Without Pulse

The second characteristic of an undead adolescent is a lack of pulse. We know that without a pulse, living beings cannot survive. A pulse is generated by the pressure of blood pushing against blood vessels (arteries and veins) as it is pumped by the heart to all areas of the body. The constraints of arteries and veins allow the blood to be channeled in the right direction to the right places. Without these channels, our blood could not be replenished with the oxygen and nutrients necessary for our bodies' survival. Instead, blood would seep out in all directions, coagulate, and be useless. Fictional zombies do not have a pulse, and neither do our teenage zombies. But in the cases of our teenagers, that pulse represents *direction*.

Undead adolescents are directionless, and this lack of direction leads them to focus all their attention on one thing: themselves. This self-centeredness, as you know, generates a great deal of conflict within the family system. Because directionless teenagers are all about instantly gratifying their own personal needs, they give no thought to the long-term consequences of their decisions or how they are impacting their present and future relationships. They have very little restraint when it comes to pleasure. When confronted with a challenge, they will often take the path of least resistance. They use things like food, video games, pornography, drugs and alcohol, and even romantic relationships with other people as a way to escape the demands of life.

What is worse is that they seem oblivious to their selfishness and to the needs of others. They are in denial. When confronted, they can become defensive and emotional, spouting off a hundred reasons for why they are right and you are wrong. When they want something, they will use circular arguments and relentless persistence to wear you down. As a result, they can suck the life out of you. Giving in to their demands so you achieve temporary peace can be a real temptation for you. But in doing so, you are robbing them of the very pulse you are trying to generate within them.

It is important to note that underlying this seeming lack of motivation, self-centeredness, and instant gratification, undead adolescents struggle with deeper issues: confusion, fear, and anger. Zombies without a pulse have no way to channel these emotions in a way that is productive. They lack the moral framework necessary to contain, direct, or restrain their passions.

A Life Without Fiber

If your teenager is motivated toward a clear purpose and is pursuing that purpose with a clear moral framework, and even if by all outward appearances he seems successful, be careful: he might still be a teenage zombie. Some zombies appear to be in control, but this control is obsessive, superficial, and fear-based. It is meant to keep an underlying emotional fragility hidden. This leads us to the third and final element that a zombie teenager lacks: fiber. We know that fibers hold the human body together: muscle fibers, ligaments, bones, cartilage, tissue, and the like. Fictional zombies lack fiber. Their bodies are depicted as rotting flesh. Many hobble around with broken or missing limbs. When the pressure reaches a certain level, they literally fall apart.

Your teenage zombie has the same problem. For him, fiber represents determination—what the ancients called fortitude. The word *fortitude* means "courage in the face of pain or adversity." The undead have an overwhelming fear of the future. Because their identity is unformed and insecure, they wonder about their capability to survive on their own. Because of this, they put a great deal of energy into controlling their circumstances. This control often looks good to parents. These zombies are usually straight-A students, star athletes, popular, service-oriented, conflict-avoidant, and all-around "good kids." But behind all of these "good" things is an obsessive fear of the future. In order to combat this fear, they must create the perfect set of circumstances to feel comfortable. Yet, with an ever-building sense of entrapment in their current circumstances—circumstances they, themselves, have often created—fiber-less zombies have a breaking point. Out of the blue, they may lash out in anger, retreat into isolation and depression, or panic and lose focus. The longer they remain paralyzed by their fear of failure, the more like the undead they become.

Fiber-less zombies may develop what psychologists call *low frustration tolerance.*[3] They cannot handle getting a B on a test, missing a shot or goal, being dumped by a boyfriend or girlfriend, or not looking like the supermodel they idolize in the magazines. Eating disorders, obsessive compulsive disorder, generalized anxiety disorder, and social phobias are common in this group. They may be shy, avoidant, or quick to please. They do not use drugs, sleep around, or get in trouble with the law. Though very successful in most things they pursue, they still don't feel that they are measuring up to the standards they or others have set for them. As a result, they rely heavily on their parents and other close relationships for validation, encouragement, and advice. This keeps them very dependent emotionally on people.

Unfortunately, many parents see their children's continual seeking of advice and reassurance as a sign of conscientiousness and diligence, not as a compulsive means of suppressing irrational fears. For those parents who can sense the fear, they cannot understand it. "What are you worried about?" parents ask,. "You're doing great!" But the teenage zombies know they're not. They are anticipating the next mistake, the next situation that might betray their weaknesses, the next shoe falling, or the next attack. They fear rejection, abandonment, and failure, so they work, they train, they achieve. Outwardly they are getting stronger, but inwardly they are wasting away. Unlike the mindless zombies, these teenagers are conscious of the passions lurking inside of them and feel true anxiety and remorse over their destructive tendencies. Knowing these tendencies, their consciences are much heightened and overbearing. Paralyzed both mentally and emotionally by the knowledge of what the beast inside of them is capable of doing, they exist in self-made prisons of fear, separated from the joys of real life.

If any of these features sound like traits within your child, you may be dealing with an undead adolescent. Don't freak out! You are not alone. The truth is that all teenagers go through an undead phase and most are resurrected successfully. To whatever degree your son or daughter is a part of the walking dead, there is hope. With education and a good survival kit, you will have the tools necessary to endure with your teen and see your teen through to the other side.

Let's review: Motivation, the spark of all life, initiates our actions. This spark is generated by our experience of two powerful sensations: pleasure and pain. These are the jumper cables that, when used together, generate the spark of motivation that moves us all.

Direction, the pulse of all life, channels our actions. This pulse is contained by our understanding and practice of two essential elements: right and wrong. Pulse is generated through the rules by which we choose to pursue pleasure and avoid pain.

Finally, determination, the fiber of all life, sustains our actions. Our fiber is strengthened by our ability to maintain a balanced perspective on two opposing forces: success and failure. The skills we possess matched against the challenges we face may determine our momentary success or failure in any given situation, but our determination will most certainly govern how we grow through both successes and failures over time.

The perfect balance between these three factors—motivation, direction, and determination—creates a flow that keeps us moving forward successfully in life.

Strategy Questions

1. After reading this first chapter, you should have a sense of the areas where your teenager is struggling. Where specifically does your son or daughter lack spark, pulse, and/or fiber in his or her life?
2. What have been the biggest challenges you've experienced in trying to generate spark, pulse, and fiber in your teenage zombie?

CHAPTER 2

The Teenage Zombie Origins

Why are we seeing so many more zombies wandering through their adolescence? Are there current trends that can help explain this uprising of the undead? One of my jobs as a psychiatrist is to look for patterns: patterns of thought, emotion, and behavior in the lives of the clients I treat. Identifying these patterns is the key to all future changes. These patterns are evident on three levels: (1) within individuals, (2) within groups of individuals, and (3) within society as a whole.

On an individual level, I witness patterns in the lives of the teenagers I see one-on-one in my private clinical practice. In my various teaching roles, I witness patterns in groups of students each year. Societal patterns are just as important to observe. They are the cultural shifts that subtly drive the popularity of books, movies, songs, art, social media, and recreational activities for the adolescent consumer. Many psychologists and philosophers have tried to observe and describe these shifts. Carl Jung called them evidence of a collective unconsciousness.[1] Making ourselves aware of these patterns gives us insight into the challenges our teenagers face and empowers us to foster positive change in their lives. I believe there is a reason why undead fantasy fiction is so popular in our culture today: it is because many of the themes depicted onscreen resonate with the struggles that adolescents and their parents face today.

What's Changed?

The developmental stage of adolescence used to be closely tied to puberty, the biological maturing process of the teenage years. Before the Industrial Revolution, children were viewed as miniature adults expected to participate in age-appropriate duties to ensure the survival of the family as a whole. In agrarian societies, this would mean helping on the farm or with household chores such as cooking and cleaning. Education was highly valued and encouraged in those who showed a clear promise of ability, and it was often coupled or replaced with an apprenticeship in some kind of trade.[2] Marriage and the bearing of children were arranged for women as soon as they were biologically able and for men as soon as they were financially able. The transition from childhood to adulthood was very short, dramatically so in many cases. Charles Dickens, the author of *Great Expectations*, describes this quick transition into adulthood through his fictitious character Pip. Having worked as a blacksmith's apprentice for over a year and now preparing to become an English gentleman, Pip reflects simply but profoundly on his last night at home: "I put my light out, and crept into bed; and it was an uneasy bed now, and I never slept the old sound sleep in it anymore."[3]

In today's culture, circumstances are much changed, but not necessarily for better or for worse. They are just different. Today's teenager faces unique challenges compared to teenagers of past generations. Today adolescence has not only become a transitional stage between childhood and adulthood, it is an increasingly ill-defined stage that can last well into a child's twenties, thirties, and even forties. Some psychologists have added a developmental stage after adolescence called "emerging adulthood."[4] Whereas in earlier societies, apprenticeships, property rights, marriages, and childbearing provided clear rites of passage into adulthood, current social and psychological stressors have contributed to the confusion, anxiety, resentment, and helplessness the modern adolescent must overcome. Below is a short list of some of the challenges with which the modern adolescent must contend.

The Nature of Work

In the past, there were more opportunities for unskilled laborers. Adolescents could begin working earlier and were expected to do so in order to help support their families. Much of the training they received was on the job. The ability to be productive and contribute to the family in a meaningful way gave adolescents a sense of direction, motivation, and confidence. These experiences were often forced upon them out of necessity; if everyone in the family did not pull their weight, the family as a whole would suffer.

Today there are several factors that have changed this dynamic. With technological advancements, many jobs that were once performed by humans are now performed by machines. This means that people must have higher levels of education in order to perform the jobs that are currently needed. More education means more time spent transitioning between dependency on the family of origin and independence as a contributing member of society.

Also, families don't rely on their children as much for income, at least in first world countries, because most households have one (if not two) parents who work outside the home and earn enough income to provide for the rest of the family. Now adolescents who are fortunate enough not to carry the burden of providing for their families have a different problem: idleness.

Adolescents who are not needed as contributing members of their families are left to determine for themselves what purpose they are going to serve. Many turn to sports as a focus. They develop skills such as discipline, perseverance, and teamwork through this venue. Others focus on their academics, developing book smarts and intellectualism through rigorous study. Many engage in forms of community service as a means of fostering a giving spirit. These are all worthwhile pursuits, but they don't often provide the well-rounded education learned through what the old-timers called "the school of hard knocks." Because most of the work done by parents is outside of the home, there is little opportunity for parents to model the skills necessary for teenagers to mature. Because of the busyness of modern society, there is barely enough time for families to connect at dinner, let alone work together side-by-side for a common cause.

As a result, adolescents have been inadvertently told by society that they are not yet ready to be a part of the real world. To compensate they have created their own subculture: one ruled by popularity, fashion, sports, video-gaming, consumerism, social media, partying, drugs, alcohol, and sex. It comes as no surprise that most marketing campaigns are geared toward teenagers and twentysomethings. This group drives pop culture.

Adolescence has become synonymous with immaturity. Though eventually most adolescents do mature and contribute to the greater good, it takes a much longer time to reach that point. In the meantime, instilling a healthy work ethic into their child's character can be a daunting challenge for many parents.

Entitlement

A seed is planted in today's adolescents that grows with them into young adulthood. The phenomenon known as a "failure to launch" is more common than you might think. Around 13 percent of adult children between the ages of eighteen and twenty-nine end up moving back with their parents after a period of time on their own.[5] There are several reasons for this failure to launch. One is financial. Especially in hard economic times, young people struggle to find good enough jobs to support themselves and pay down the high debts they've incurred from increasingly expensive and lengthening educations.

But the problem goes deeper than financial necessity. According to the World Bank, the United States is the eighth wealthiest country in the world.[6,7] It is certainly one of the most powerful. Advances in technology have made the world's resources more accessible to young people motivated to succeed than at any other time in history. Unfortunately, many American adolescents seem unwilling or incapable of using these resources to succeed in life. As is the case for any generation growing up in an affluent society, a young person's sense of entitlement can become a major hindrance to his or her success. Many adult children have little appreciation for the sacrifices the previous generations have made for their comfort. Naturally, they balk at the idea of working for something they have always gotten for free. Comparing the physical, social, and psychological problems of past generations with the modern comforts we enjoy, it might reasonably be said that we have become weaker as a society. I am not alone in this sentiment:

> Researchers suggest that Generation Y has an inflated sense of self-esteem that clashes unpleasantly with the harsh realities of the modern world. Kids grow up believing that they're special, talented, and can be anything they want to be, and when that doesn't always pan out, they easily fall into chronic disappointment and despair. In essence, the idea seems to be that if they cannot have exactly what they want, there is little point in trying; rather than working relentlessly toward their goals, these entitled youngsters simply give up.[8]

Social Isolation

If it were just an issue of young adults living at home longer, parents might be able to adapt. In fact, launching of the modern individual from his or her family of origin is actually a more recent, Western phenomenon. Many societies still maintain and encourage multigenerational households where parents, grandparents, and even aunts, uncles, and cousins live and work together, providing for the good of the family as a whole.

Unfortunately, this alone is not the problem. The modern adolescent's psychological problems have become increasingly prevalent and debilitating. These add additional strain to the family far beyond the financial and housing burdens parents assume.

For example, many young people have become increasingly

isolated from their peer groups as technology replaces face-to-face communication. We live in a world where breakups occur over text messages. Exciting life events are announced on Facebook. We see people's lives progress through a series of pictures on Instagram and Snapchat. Communication occurs through pithy sentences devoid of verbal tone or expressive body language. It is no wonder that many adolescents are socially inept and extremely lonely, struggling to break free from the family of origin with whom they feel most comfortable.[9]

I spoke with a prominent businessman recently who told me that young professionals, fresh out of school, are needing to be trained on how to communicate effectively on an emotional level with clients. He said that they have been so used to communicating via texts and social media, that when confronted with real, live people, they have no idea what to say or how to act. As a result of poor communication, companies can lose a great deal of business.

Many studies are being performed on the effects of social media on depression. The virtual realities generated online set people up for disappointment when their mundane lives don't appear to measure up to the adventures depicted on their screens.

Social psychologists have also likened excessive online connectivity to the obesity epidemic. Both are the result of too much of a good thing.[10] Think about it. In all ways, humans have a natural inclination to make life easier by taking things we need and making them more accessible. In the case of food, we have manufactured calorie-rich products that are easily and quickly consumed but fail to provide sustainable energy. As a result, we end up feeling more lethargic, remain sedentary, and face an increase in weight and a loss of overall physical ability.

A similar phenomenon occurs with social media. We all have a need to feel connected, but online connections are to sustainable relationships what Krispy Kreme donuts are to sustainable nourishment. They are easy, cheap, and feel amazing, but they are poor substitutes for the real thing. Many adolescents who are growing up with social media as their primary form of connection do not have the skills or the desire to engage in healthier, albeit harder and messier, forms of connection with others. Depression sets in when adolescents realize that their online connections are all superficial and nothing more than fluff. Scrolling through a Facebook, Twitter, or Instagram feed on a Saturday night and seeing all the happy pictures of digitized lives and comparing them to your own can be a very depressing experience. Many teenagers develop the sense that their whole life should be one big, fun, and exciting event after another. They fail to realize that much of life is routine, hard work.

The Paradox of Choice

Most parents believe that if they create the right social environment for their children and place before them every potential opportunity for success, then their children can do nothing but succeed and be happy. Unfortunately, studies have shown that affluence is not as much of a protective factor against mental suffering as we once thought.[11] In fact, the more choices available to an individual, the more likely they are to struggle with anxiety and regret over making the wrong choice.[12]

It may be that young people feel overwhelmed by the opportunities they have. They face tremendous pressure to make something of themselves and respond in various ways. Some shut down in the face of pressure, choosing instead to distract themselves with more immediate and attainable rewards. As a result, they may appear to have little or no motivation for success. Others cannot seem to decide on a direction for their education or career. They feel too confused and paralyzed to act.

According to the Bureau of Labor Statistics, the participation of young people in the workforce has been steadily declining since the late 1980s. With July being the peak month for teen employment, 2013 saw a 17-point drop in participation rates of young people ages sixteen to twenty-four compared to the same month in 1989.[13] For those who do work, they will hold an average of seven to eight different jobs between the ages of eighteen and thirty. One out of every four of these individuals will have more than ten jobs during this period.[14] Many young people today believe there is a "right" job that will make them feel happy and fulfilled. Rather than sticking with a position for an extended duration, they change jobs until one feels right to them. Many teenagers have taken this mind-set into all activities of life. Those activities that fail to provide instant gratification are often scrapped for those activities that have the most immediate and biggest "bang for the buck."

"Not-So-Free" Expression

Many adolescents struggle with emotional intelligence—the knowledge of and ability to communicate one's own emotions. This is made worse by the fact that most teenagers today do not self-reflect before seeking validation for their feelings from peers. In therapy I will often have individuals write letters to themselves or to others, expressing the emotions they feel about a given situation. I always tell them not to send the letter until we have had a chance to read it and process it together. This helps with the important steps of self-understanding and self-soothing. Self-soothing is the ability to talk one's self through his or her own emotional states and find comfort without the help of others. In the past, the ability to self-soothe was a sign of a maturing adult. But today many teenagers do not spend enough time in self-reflection. They immediately post what they are thinking, feeling, or doing for all to see on the Internet. This free expression does actually have a cost.

The first cost is a loss of intimacy. Sharing used to be a key feature of an intimate relationship. Now you find out about your best friend's acceptance to college or your classmates' weekend getaway over the Internet, along with their seven hundred other friends. The definition of intimacy has changed.

The second is a loss of discretion. When we post online, we have limited control over who sees what we write. This leaves us vulnerable to scrutiny, criticism, judgment, and distancing, most of which we never feel or know directly. Our teens' online expressions are being read by their peers. Because of the anonymity the Internet provides, we can never be sure of the impressions and attitudes that are being formed by those who read our posts. Followers can voyeuristically read these expressions without facing the responsibility of reacting or confronting them. They can simply keep on scrolling and the individual who posted never gets the helpful, although possibly critical, feedback she or he would have gotten through a face-to-face interaction. Those who do give negative feedback are often labeled as "haters" and can be unfriended or blocked.

As a result, teenagers face a third problem: unbalanced feedback. Adolescents can carefully select those peers who engage their posts to find the affirmation they crave. Think about it: we know that our identity is in part defined by the groups with which we interact. However, the more control I have over the dynamics of the group I engage, the more likely the group will be a mirrored version of myself. If this is true and I am unaware of it, then any understanding I have of myself is an illusion generated by my own fantasy reality. Like the Smiths in *The Matrix*, I can simply morph every online encounter into a reflected version of my desires. This can have a profound impact on my ability to empathize with others and to form healthy relationships with people who think differently than I do.

"Free" expression online can have other damaging effects on the recipients as well. Cyber-bullying has become an epidemic, leaving many young people traumatized and unsure of their self-worth moving into the world. Without a physical presence to moderate interactions, people often feel free to say whatever they want without direct consequences or even an awareness of the hurt they inflict on others.[15]

Fatal Attractions

The challenge of forming a healthy sexual and gender identity has become more difficult due to ambiguity in the definitions of masculinity and femininity.[16] Some would argue that this ambiguity is good, that men and women really are not that different after all. However, anyone who has ever been an adolescent (which would be all of us) knows how difficult it is to understand his or her own sexuality and gender identity without the help of established guidelines. Unfortunately, today's teenagers are bombarded from all directions by family, friends, teachers, books, movies, television shows, music, and advertisements with messages about what it means to be a man and what it means to be a woman. Inherent in these definitions are messages on how a man and a woman are to interact with each other. Without clear boundaries and guidelines, adolescents can get themselves into serious trouble.

The challenge of finding a romantic partner starts in the adolescent years. It is one of the most stressful experiences of this stage of development. Currently, the average age that young people marry is at an all-time high (age twenty-five for women and twenty-seven for men). Whether this delay of marriage is a cause or an effect of premarital sexual intercourse, statistics show that 80 percent of young adults have had sex prior to marriage and that many practice what sociologists call *serial monogamy*— multiple shorter-term romantic relationships that include sexual intercourse.[17] Unfortunately, many young people realize too late how complicated sex is psychologically. Multiple relationships and breakups can heighten the distrust of future partners, foster comparisons between past and present relationships, lower self-confidence and esteem, decrease current relationship satisfaction, and provoke greater anxiety over whether or not their final choice—the partner with whom they commit to in marriage—is the "right" one. The 50 percent divorce rate in America does not help to encourage faith in the institution either. Still, cohabitation can be just as stressful, if not more so. Women especially wrestle with the possibility that years spent in a serious, but uncommitted, relationship could end in a breakup, leaving them closer to the end of their childbearing years and at the mercy of a society where it is more acceptable for men to marry much younger partners.

Divorced and blended families pose unique challenges. Studies have shown that children from divorced families are at higher risk of academic problems, using drugs and alcohol, and experiencing depression.[18] Relationships with stepfamilies are often fraught with conflict and resentments.[19]

Indecent Exposure

Adolescence is usually the stage when young people are exposed to the abuse of drugs and alcohol, as well as other behaviors that can quickly turn into compulsions. This only complicates the difficulties parents have in launching their children successfully into the world. The following is just a sampling of the current data we have available.

Drugs and Alcohol

The National Institute on Drug Abuse reports:

In 2013, 7.0 percent of 8th graders, 18.0 percent of 10th graders, and 22.7 percent of 12th graders used marijuana in the past month, up from 5.8 percent, 13.8 percent, and 19.4 percent in 2008. Daily use has also increased; 6.5 percent of 12th graders now use marijuana every day, compared to 5 percent in the mid-2000s. . . . In 2013, 15.0 percent of high school seniors used a prescription drug non-medically in the past year . . . In 2013, 3.5 percent of 8th graders, 12.8 percent of 10th graders, and 26 percent of 12th graders reported getting drunk in the past month.[20]

Video Games

The American Medical Association reports that "up to 90 percent of American youth play video games. Of those teens and young adults, it's speculated that up to 15 percent may be addicted."[21]

Cutting

Self-injury is on the rise in America. Though it has been hard to quantify the exact statistics, lifetime prevalence rates for adolescents within the community range from 15 to 20 percent.[22] These numbers are higher for those under the care of a mental health professional. Self-injurious behaviors can include more than just cutting. The DSM-V has now created distinct categories for trichotillomania (hair pulling) and dermatillomania (skin picking). Other behaviors include tattooing, burning, piercing, and embedding, which is the placement of various items under the skin. According to a study performed by researchers at Cornell University, approximately one in five college students has participated in some form of self-injury. The majority of cutters are female, but males do engage in the behavior as well. Most individuals who self-injure will report that they do so as a means of increasing their sense of control over their circumstances and freeing themselves from emotional numbness.

Eating Disorders

Anorexia is the third most common chronic illness among adolescents.[23] The pressure to maintain an idealized weight leads more than half of teenage girls and a third of teenage boys to use unhealthy practices to control their weight, including cigarette smoking, purging with laxatives or self-induced vomiting, excessive exercise, or self-starvation.[24]

Pornography

According to the website Covenant Eyes, 93 percent of boys and 62 percent of girls have been exposed to Internet pornography before the age of eighteen.[25] According to the Internet Filter Review, the largest consumer of Internet pornography is the twelve to seventeen age group.[26]

First Breaks

Young adults are not immune to mental illness either. First breaks of psychosis, depression, anxiety, and other chronic mental illnesses like bipolar disorder and schizophrenia surface in the teens and twenties. According to the Centers for Disease Control, suicide is the third leading cause of death in young people ages ten to twenty-four. Approximately 4,600 adolescents are lost to suicide each year in the United States. Approximately 157,000 are treated in emergency rooms each year for suicide attempts.[27] "A nationwide survey of youth in grades 9–12 in public and private schools in the United States (U.S.) found that 16 percent of students reported seriously considering suicide, 13 percent reported creating a plan, and 8 percent reported trying to take their own life in the 12 months preceding the survey."[28]

When you add together all mental disorders generally, which would include major depressive disorder (MDD), generalized anxiety disorder (GAD), obsessive compulsive disorder (OCD), attention deficit hyperactivity disorder (ADHD), bipolar disorder, and schizophrenia, the National Institute on

Mental Health reports that one in five children ages thirteen to eighteen "either currently or at some point in their life have had a severe, debilitating mental disorder." If you remove the term "severe" from the definition, lifetime prevalence of a mental disorder in this age group rises to 50 percent.[29] Fifty percent! That is staggering.

With all of these challenges facing adolescents and emerging adults, it is no wonder that moving forward through this ever-lengthening stage of development has become almost impossible for many teens. But there is hope. It is only the unseen and unprepared for dangers that can kill us. If we know what we are fighting, we will be better equipped to defeat it—or in this case, resurrect it.

In the following chapters, we will explore the nature and characteristics of teenage zombies so that we may understand their hearts, their brains, and their spirits. This knowledge will give us a framework for applying the best tactics available to bring life back to the undead.

————— Strategy Questions —————

1. How do you think society and the cultural environment in which you live have affected the zombification of your teenager?
2. How have you become discouraged in your parenting? What tools would you like to gain from reading this book?

CHAPTER 3

The Teenage Zombie Brain

If you have a teenage zombie living in your home, you know that teenage zombies often do things that do not make sense to us adults. It is very easy to get frustrated with their lack of attention, their volatile emotions, and their impulsive and defiant decisions. In this chapter, we will talk about some of the biological factors that influence and contend with your son's or daughter's motivation, direction, and determination in life. This is not a simple black-and-white, cause-and-effect relationship. A zombie adolescent's brain is quite complex, but when an adolescent's emotions and behaviors appear random and inexplicable to you, it can be helpful to consider how his or her brain works. The more insight you have, the calmer your own nerves will be (literally), allowing for more rational responses to the conflicts you have with your teenager.

Science has given us clues to understand some of the physiological mechanisms that drive adolescent behavior. We now know that the adolescent brain undergoes dramatic changes before it reaches maturity. To stay calm and act rationally, we must understand that not all of this is their fault. The way teenagers' brains develop over time has a significant effect on their attitudes and actions. If we can understand this (even when they do not), we will be able to do three things:

1. foster experiences for our teenagers that will have a positive impact on their memories of adolescence and help motivate them toward independence;
2. create boundaries that will help to contain their thoughts, emotions, and actions in a way that avoids permanent physical, psychological, and spiritual damage; and
3. provide an appropriate balance of encouragement and challenge at a level that matches the skill and life experience our children possess.

To accomplish these three tasks, we must start from the beginning of our children's brain development and understand from a biological perspective how they became the way they are right now. It starts with *nature versus nurture*. You have heard this expression before, I am sure. It basically means that there are some characteristics our teenagers are born with and some that develop over time through exposure to the environment around them. Let's explore both for just a moment.

Nature and Nurture

The nature of a teenage zombie represents the foundational characteristics with which he or she was born. For example, your child's brain starts out with the basic building blocks necessary for sensing pleasure and pain.

A child knows intuitively what his basic needs are. He does not have to be told when he is hungry, tired, hot, cold, injured, uncomfortable, or content. He also knows intuitively how to meet his needs. Unfortunately, there is only one way at first: crying. A child's cry is his first interaction with the environment, his first means of attaining a reward or avoiding pain. How that cry is answered by the environment becomes the baby's first experience of nurturing. A caretaker's response to a child's cry begins the process of influencing the child's motivation (spark), direction (pulse), and determination (fiber) for life.

As your child grows, this dynamic of your responsiveness to his needs coupled with your and your child's basic dispositions has been, in part, responsible for molding him into the person he is today. Of course, there are other environmental issues that affect your child's development that are out of your control: other relationships and other life events, good and bad. Early on, however, you are most responsible for the environments to which your child is exposed.

Now, we cannot go back and change the past. We all recognize that our actions as parents may have had an impact on the current undead state of our children. It is easy to let guilt overwhelm us. I will deal with this in a future chapter, but for now, realize that it is never too late to nurture your teenage zombie in a positive way. Here are some helpful tips to do so.

Understand His Basic Personality

Who does he most resemble or take after? Who in the family does he normally confide in? Who does he have the most fun with? What are his hobbies and interests? How can you foster these pursuits and use them as teachable moments to instill deeper truths and passions? What are his inherent struggles? Does he get discouraged easily? Are they too complacent? Is he strong-willed and rebellious? Is he difficult to read? Taking time to understand his basic personality will give you wisdom on how to approach him when you want to influence him in a positive direction.

Know His Limitations

How much can he really handle? What is his current level of performance in school, sports, and other extracurricular activities? How emotionally intelligent is he? Where is he facing discouragement and fear that is holding him back? If you are pushing a child too far, he will eventually break. Understanding the challenges he is facing each day and providing reasonable expectations will stimulate his motivation, keep him moving forward no matter how slowly in the right direction, and build fiber in his character as he starts to see small successes in his life.

Create Scaffolding[1]

If you look at a building under construction, the scaffolding is always just beyond the structure of the building itself. As the building expands, so does the scaffolding. This is a helpful way of looking at your child's development. For example, if your son is currently failing in school, don't expect him to get straight As. Provide helpful encouragement when he passes his classes. Once he starts passing, then you can up the ante and require Bs or As for further reward.

The key is to help your son see that he is capable of what you require of him. If the mountain before him seems insurmountable, you have to help him reach lower summits. This is not just true for achievements, but emotionally as well. If your son struggles with his temperament, give him the tools necessary to overcome this and build him up when he has little successes.

Know Your Hot Buttons (Your Kids Sure Do)

You should be able to anticipate the actions of your teenagers that drive you up a wall. Prepare for them mentally as much as is possible. The goal is to stay calm, be prepared for anything, and remain in the battle, knowing that perseverance will produce the desired character you'd like to see in your kids. Seeing that character develop will give you hope for their future without you.

Create Memories that Foster the Motivation, Direction, and Determination You Wish for in Your Kids

Memory, as we will see, has a profound impact on how we see ourselves, our relationships, the world around us, and the future. In the midst of difficult times with your kids, anything you can do to create positive memories for them to cling to in the future will help them to avoid discouragement later on. For example, one father I know who was struggling to connect with his son bought a 1969 Ford Mustang to restore. Every Saturday morning, he and his son would work on it together. During that time, all conflict was set aside as they focused on the task at hand. Eventually, it became a time for father and son to talk about the hard things of life: the parents' divorce, the dad's struggle with his family of origin, the son's questions and fears about girls. The car became a metaphor for the son as he grew older. It represented to him the reality that, in life, we can get pretty beat up, but if you keep working on yourself, no matter how bad things get, you can always be restored. His dad wasn't perfect, but that memory forever imprinted on his brain stuck with him long after his father passed away.

Neuronal Connectors

We talked about the process of nature and nurture—now let's talk more specifically about how the human brain develops. The human brain is not a static processor. With repeated exposures to stimuli over time, the brain begins to process information differently. It adapts. This process occurs through the formation of neuronal connections in the developing brain.

Neurons are the basic cellular structures that form the human brain and nervous system and are responsible for transporting information necessary for the body to function properly. Without neurons, we cannot think, feel, or act. Neurons allow us to sense the environment; process, synthesize, and interpret the information received; and then tell the body how to respond. In addition, neurons are responsible for the storage of information—memory—to be accessed efficiently when a familiar situation requires it.

The more often a signal is passed between two neurons, the tighter the bond that develops between them. This makes it more likely that future signals will travel by this path of least resistance, much like a well-worn tire track. Scientists have described this hardwiring with the saying, "Neurons that fire together wire together."[2] With 100 billion neurons, each having 10,000 branches, the potential for different connections between neurons is unfathomable. This is where the nurturing of the environment has an influence. The basic genetic elements of the neurons when coupled with repeated exposures to the environment establish the connections in the brain that become the basis of our personality—the structural framework by which we understand and engage the world around us.

Pruning and Hardwiring

The development of this structural framework of the human brain—the wiring of neuronal connections based on repeated exposure to the environment—is a process that continues well into the second and third decades of life. Brain imaging studies show that various parts of the human brain undergo rapid growth at different times, followed by a process known as pruning. Pruning occurs when neuronal pathways rarely being used are trimmed away, making the brain more efficient at sending information via more strongly established neuronal routes. Like the pruning away of dead branches from a tree, the remaining branches have less competition and grow stronger.

Your son is still making connections between his memories, his physiology, his relationships, and his psychological understanding of pleasure and pain. The pruning process weeds out those signals that create dissonance in your teenager's understanding and experience of the world.

When the brain has established a connection that leads to a predictable response, we call it hardwiring. Hardwiring explains why we tend to think, feel, and act in predictable patterns over time. These behaviors require little conscious effort. They happen naturally. It also explains why we tend to form connections with people who reinforce patterns we learned in our past. Your child's choices in friends, favorite teachers, coaches, bosses, or romantic partners are influenced by past experiences with people. Unconsciously, we will gravitate toward the familiar. Your zombie teenager may not be able to explain why he acted the way he did, but his brain knows. It's all in his hardwiring.

Why is this important for you as the parent to understand? Well, to begin with, each subsequent experience your child has in life builds on the one he had before. This means that it is absolutely necessary for parents to be intentional about the kinds of experiences their children have and to help their teenagers interpret them in the right way. It is not necessary or possible for a parent to shield a child from all painful experiences and only provide pleasurable experiences in life. Instead, continual dialogue with a child about both can help shape his perspective, create hardwiring that is effective in dealing with emotional challenges, and protect him from further trauma by teaching him how to react to similar future scenarios.

Second, the way a parent models an appropriate response to the environment can shape a teenager's understanding and actions in a similar way. When your teenager observes your successes and mistakes and sees you working on your own development, he can learn vicariously through you. Many parents believe they have to have it all together mentally, emotionally, and spiritually in order to raise healthy kids, but a child's hardwiring develops as much through observing their parents' failures as well as successes.

Finally, realize that although hardwiring does predispose someone to predictable patterns of thought, emotion, and behavior, this hardwiring is still flexible. It is possible for someone to change over time. The point is this: never lose hope. No matter how broken your relationship with your teenage zombie may be, it is never too late to influence him positively. Any situation is redeemable. I had a client who struggled with severe depression for most of her children's early years of development. She was often in bed sleeping, unable to care for her kids. Because of this, she battled the guilt and shame of not being a good parent for many years. However, she recently consented to start medication for her depression and has noticed a world of difference. Her children have seen that difference also and have found some comfort in knowing now what their mother suffered through those years. They have also found strength in her humility to reach out for help and have exhibited that same humility in their own lives. Because of their mother's difficulties while they were growing up, they have developed a strong resilience that is serving them well in life. Do they still have issues to work through? Of course, but that is true of everyone. The point is that progress, not perfection, is the goal. If you can understand this with your zombie teenager, you will be better equipped to help him navigate this stage of confusion and change.

The Speed of Development

Although hardwiring is a process that occurs all throughout the developing brain, it does not occur at the same speed in all regions of the brain. It is also not the only process that must occur in a teenager's brain in order for it to develop fully. The speed at which signals are transmitted in the brain is determined in part by the thickness of insulation surrounding the nerve fibers. Myelin is a sheath that surrounds the neurons, insulating them and allowing for the faster transmission of signals, much like the plastic sheaths that surround the electrical wiring in our homes. Myelination, the process of insulating neurons, occurs gradually at different times and places within the developing brain well into a person's twenties. This process of myelination may explain some of the impulsive, emotionally driven actions of an adolescent. To consider how, we must explain the structure and function of some important regions of the brain.

The brain is divided into three main regions. The brain stem is the area of the brain that regulates breathing and wakefulness. Surrounding the brain stem is the midbrain, which contains structures collectively known as the limbic system. These structures regulate our basic human drives, such as sleep, sexual arousal, hunger, thirst, and emotional memory and reactivity. The outermost layer of the brain is called the cortex. This part of the brain synthesizes all the signals received by the brain, formulates plans based on those signals, executes the plans, and then evaluates the effectiveness of the actions taken, making changes where necessary. The area of the cortex located near the front of the brain is called the prefrontal cortex (PFC). This area of the brain allows for metacognition—our ability to think about thinking. This ability to self-reflect is one of the features that distinguishes us from the fictitious zombies in stories.

Scientists have found that outer, analytically driven regions of the brain like the PFC take longer to myelinate than the deeper, emotionally driven regions of the brain like the limbic system.[3] This may explain why adolescents literally act without thinking. Compared to an adult brain, an adolescent brain's deeper emotionally driven limbic system works more efficiently than the higher, executive functioning cortex. This can lead to unrestrained emotional responses to environmental stimuli as opposed to well-thought-out reactions.

Even if you cannot remember what it was like to be a young, headstrong adolescent, you might be able to relate to teenagers' impulsive, emotional reactivity when you consider your own responses to sudden stressors. Even in a brain whose higher cortical brain regions are fully myelinated, the reactive fight-or-flight response, which is regulated by the deeper structures of the limbic system, can override the system. In these moments of sudden intense stress, distress signals bypass our higher executive brain regions and cause us to act "without thinking"! Such is the case when we get cut off suddenly in traffic, get spooked by shadows in the night, or get called unexpectedly to the human resources office at work. Our body reacts without thinking. Our heart rate increases, our eyes dilate, our palms sweat, and our stomach churns. Fortunately, as adults, our PFC kicks in pretty quickly and allows us to maintain our cool in most situations, but this is much harder for an adolescent.

Hopefully, the more you are aware of these developmental changes taking place within your adolescent's brain, the more clarity, patience, and wisdom you have in molding his life experiences, teaching him healthy boundaries, and exhibiting grace and empathy while still training him up in the direction he should be headed.

Environmental Influences

From the moment of conception, your child's biology is being influenced by the physical world. As your child matures, these chemical influences will continue to have an effect. When puberty starts, young people have to insert meaning into new biological pleasures and pains they have never felt before. Hormonal changes have an impact on their sexuality, appetite, sleep cycle, emotions, and energy levels. You may have noticed that your adolescent's drive for food increased dramatically during this stage of their development. Many parents of adolescents have lamented over the size of their grocery bill. They must also determine how to satisfy the sexual drive that heightens during this stage, a fact that some parents would prefer to ignore. Even an adolescent's sleep requirements and cycles change, leaving parents exhausted by late-night talks. In early adolescence, girls begin their menstrual cycles, experiencing monthly shifts in the balance of estrogen and progesterone, accounting for the moodiness, irritability, and emotional volatility often seen. We think of teenagers as having "raging hormones." For boys in particular, this is literally true as testosterone surges increase sex drive, aggression, risk-taking behaviors, and dominance struggles within peer groups.

Though it is possible to overreact as parents, we do need to be mindful of our children's diets, the amount of exercise they are getting, their sleeping habits, the kinds of supplements they are taking, the possibility of experimentation with drugs and alcohol, and even addictive behavioral activities such as excessive time on social media, playing video games, use of pornography, or even binge-watching Netflix. The reason this is important is because the chemicals and experiences that your children introduce to their brains during this crucial stage of development can have an impact on the regulation of their natural brain chemicals, called neurotransmitters. These neurotransmitters include substances like dopamine, norepinephrine, serotonin, glutamate, and acetylcholine. The balance of these chemicals can be thrown off when dangerous substances or unhealthy activities are introduced.

Regulating your children's exposure to the environment around them is the source of most conflict between parents and children. It can be exhausting to try to maintain consistency in the face of their constant pushback, but it is important to work hard at it. Without this protection, your children's brains are at risk of serious damage. There are ways to help your teenagers make wise choices in these areas. Set limits on the use of media and encourage other activities such as art, exercise, music, reading, and creativity in their spare time. Be willing to spend money in these areas so that your kids will feel supported in their particular talents or abilities. Use less productive activities like playing video games as rewards for more engaging activities. Have a no-tolerance policy for the use of illicit substances or underage drinking, and make sure there are clear consequences for such behaviors. If you are suspicious that your child may be experimenting, ask a professional or a trusted friend to help you recognize the signs and know how to confront your adolescent appropriately.

I've told parents in my office that drug screens should be performed regularly and randomly for all teenagers, not as a form of suspicion or punishment, but as a routine requirement of being a productive member of the household, much like employees are required at a job. This takes away a teenager's ability to accuse you of distrust or "being unfair." In the end, the goal of all this regulating is really for his own health and well-being, even if he cannot see or understand it right now.

You may have to accept being the bad guy for a time in order to protect your son from himself. Establishing a treatment contract can be a good way to help your teenager feel a part of the process. By allowing him some say in the rules you create and their consequences, he will be less able to argue with you when it comes time to discipline. Treatment contracts should be as specific as possible. If you are not sure how to create one, or if the one you have established doesn't seem to be working, seek advice from a trusted mentor or counselor. Many family therapists are trained in how to help parents and children create contracts like these that establish healthy boundaries within the family system. Utilize these resources as much as you need to.

A Word about Mental Illness and Prescription Drugs

The teenage years are when many mental illnesses first manifest themselves. As parents, we must be aware that mental illness is real and, if left untreated, can lead to a downward spiral of discouragement, helplessness, and destructive behaviors that further paralyze our teenagers and make lasting recovery very difficult. I've often wondered about the hesitancy parents have in getting a son or daughter help in this area. Several reasons come to mind.

The first is confusion: many parents struggle to understand the difference between normal teenage angst and a true mental illness. *Maybe this is normal,* is a thought that has kept many families out of therapists' or psychiatrists' offices for a long time. There is also confusion about what the diagnosis of depression, anxiety, or bipolar disorder, for example, really means. This coupled with the confusion surrounding the use of prescription drugs, especially when the use of illicit substances is known to be so dangerous, makes parents skittish to seek outside help.

Cost is another factor. Many families cannot afford to obtain the kind of psychiatric or psychological care that their son or daughter needs to get well.

Third, the stigma associated with mental illness keeps many parents away, as does the fear that professionals who are not thorough in their evaluations will overprescribe medication for their kids. These fears and concerns are not unwarranted, but there are a number of steps parents can take to feel confident that they are making the right decisions to help their teenagers.

Know the Difference

Most teenagers have normal ups and downs. They can be irritable, argumentative, gloomy, and unmotivated at times. At other times, they may be giddy with excitement, productive, helpful, and kind. Concerns should start to rise when a teenager has a distinct shift in personality that lasts longer than a few days. Most psychiatric disorders require symptoms to be present for several weeks before the diagnosis can be made.

In addition to the length of time conditions have been present, an individual's level of functioning is assessed. Someone can be struggling with sadness or depression but still be able to go to school, get decent grades, participate in extracurricular activities, and enjoy pleasurable experiences such as time with friends. Concerns should arise when these daily experiences are harder and harder to perform. When individuals stop caring for themselves, isolate from friends, fail school assignments, or skip activities, these are warning signs that there is a bigger problem.

Know Your Family's Mental Health History

If you had parents, siblings, or extended family who struggled with mental illness, then it is genetically more likely that your teenagers' symptoms may be the result of something similar.

Keep an Open Dialogue

I did a radio interview recently in which a parent expressed concerns that her daughter was severely depressed. It was the start of her senior year, and she did not seem excited about it at all. In fact, she did not appear to be motivated to do much of anything. The parent was concerned about her daughter but was afraid to express those concerns. She wondered if her daughter would push her away if she approached her to talk about these issues. My response was this: if you are motivated by love and genuine concern for your daughter, then you cannot fear being pushing away. Perfect love casts out fear. There is no harm in talking to your child about what he is dealing with, expressing your concerns, and allowing him to affirm or allay those fears. If you don't ask, you will never know.

Do Your Research on Providers

Be sure to find a professional who will be thorough, taking all your questions and concerns into account, and then spend an appropriate amount of time educating you on the process and the potential treatment plan. If you know of someone who had a good experience with a provider, ask for a recommendation. Then get a second opinion or even a third or fourth, for that matter. Remember the old adage, "There is wisdom in a multitude of counselors."[4] Your son's mental health is worth the due diligence to find the person who is right for him.

Have Healthy Expectations of the Benefits of Medication and a Healthy Fear of Side Effects

I always tell my clients, medications do not cure! If you meet anyone who tells you they do, run the other way. That being said, medications are an extremely helpful tool to break a downward spiral so you can get to the positive mental place where you can face your fears and take the steps necessary to get help. Also, many of the fears people have about prescription side effects are unfounded. Common side effects can usually be managed effectively, and the majority of side effects disappear when the medication is stopped. If you're hesitant, allow yourself time to discuss your concerns with your health care provider. Any competent provider should be able to sit with you and explain the pros and cons clearly.

Consider Alternatives to Medication

Certain mental illnesses must be treated with medication, especially those in which the individual is at risk of harming himself or another person. However, there are other nonpharmacological treatments that have been shown to be effective in treating mental illness, especially depression and anxiety. Talk therapy, the process of meeting with a counselor to discuss your thoughts, emotions, and actions, has been demonstrated to be very helpful. Cognitive behavioral therapy and offshoots of this therapy have studies backing their effectiveness as well.

When looking for a counselor, examine what his style of therapy entails, how often he plans to meet with your son, what kinds of clients he works with most often, and how comfortable he feels addressing the issues your son is wrestling with. Cultural issues are also important to consider. Does he understand your child's religious background, sexual orientation, ethnicity, and gender issues? A few appointments with several therapists is not uncommon to find the right fit for you and your child.

Also realize that family therapy is just as important as individual therapy. Though your son may be the one struggling to function, you will also need help navigating his struggle. Don't be ashamed to meet as a family or on your own with a proactive therapist who will challenge you to consider areas where you might be able to change your dealings with your child. Though it may be humbling, the advantages far outweigh the disadvantages.

Now that we have had a chance to talk about the teenager's brain and discuss some of the biological factors that are influencing the development of an adolescent, it is time to shift to the heart. In the next chapter, I will address the psychological impact that relationships have on the adolescent's zombie state, along with some ways in which you can relate to your child in order to resurrect him.

Strategy Questions

1. What have you learned about your teenager's brain in this chapter that might allow you to have empathy for his or her struggle? How can you use that empathy to temper your responses to his or her unpredictable behavior at times?

2. Where in your teenager's life do you need to set limits in order to protect his or her developing brain? List several ideas you have to create those limits, and then process them with your spouse or a trusted friend, mentor, or counselor.

CHAPTER 4

The Teenage Zombie Heart

The brain is not the only part of a zombie teenager that is deadened. A teenage zombie's heart also needs to be reawakened to the joy of healthy relationships. The heart, in this context, represents the attributes that make us relational beings, the psychology that connects us to or distances us from the love of others. Unfortunately, bad experiences with people can deaden our hearts and taint our perspective on people.

I spoke to a teenage client, Derek, recently who said, "If somebody messes with me, I don't even care. I mean, I'll go off on them. I'm like, 'Who do you think you are, telling me what to do? You don't even know who I am. Why should I listen to you?' I mean, like, I'll be respectful and all as long as they're reasonable or whatever, but I don't have to listen if I don't think it's right." Here was a zombie teenager who had been betrayed by the most important authority figure in his life—his father. As a result, his attitude toward all those in authority became one of distrust and defiance. Unfortunately, this young man's attitude was not only ostracizing him from classmates, but was getting him into more trouble than necessary with his teachers on an almost daily basis. He had developed a bad reputation. His confrontational attitude with authority figures often escalated to the point of conflict, which also increased his punishments and his resentment and distrust of others. It was a downward spiral into an undead state of existence.

Another teenager, Ashley, said, "I don't see the big deal about oral sex. I mean, there is no chance that you can get pregnant. Besides, it's just fun. It doesn't have to be a serious thing. I think guys kinda expect it at some point if you're gonna mess around at a party or something." Here was a zombie teenager who had developed a flippant attitude about sexual activity. This attitude arose after her first serious boyfriend pressured her to do something that went against her family's morals. To protect herself from shame, she adopted a casual attitude about oral sex, minimizing the psychological consequences of the experiences she had had with guys. Her parents had no idea about her newly developed philosophy or the number of guys she had been with in this way: six to be precise.

Because teenagers are still forming their own identity while simultaneously working to understand the shifting identities of their peers, there is a lot of room for confusion, mistakes, misunderstandings, and deep heart wounds. You must understand these influences on your teenager's heart and work to instill within her a right attitude when relationships become painful.

Interestingly, one of the best ways you can model an appropriate response to difficult relationships for your teen is by working tirelessly to have a positive relationship with your own difficult child!

The Response of an Undead Heart

To help teenage zombies reawaken their hearts to healthy relationships, we must first understand how the undead respond to difficult relationships. They usually have one of two extreme fight-or-flight responses.

First, they fight to control people's perceptions of them by conforming to peer pressure or by embracing perfectionism. These responses allow for immediate acceptance but with a long-term cost: a lost identity that leaves them confused about who they are and what they really want. This makes them vulnerable to the control of other people who really don't care about them.

This was the case with Ashley. She felt pressured to be intimate with her boyfriend, fearful that he would break up with her if she did not please him. That same pressure continued in her other relationships.

Second, they fly from relationships by isolating from their peers or embracing the shell of an "I couldn't care less about you" attitude. These responses allow for immediate escape from the pain of people's rejection, but it blinds them from seeing the longer-term rewards of enduring difficult relationships—namely, the joy of loving and being loved in a tried and true, fully transparent relationship. This was Derek's experience. He had been betrayed by his father, so he made it his mission to be as ugly as he could to those around him. His anger, deep down, was a protection against the pain of further rejection. Ashley's casual attitude about sex was a similar protection.

Though either extreme will deaden your child's ability to form and maintain healthy relationships, they are the responses that seem most reasonable and satisfying to a zombie teenager in the moment. A controlling teenager may believe, *If I can just figure out what I need to do to be good enough, cool enough, funny enough, helpful enough, or attractive enough, this person I want a relationship with will have to want me too!*

Conversely, an escaping teenager may believe, *I will never be good enough, cool enough, funny enough, or powerful enough to gain this desirable person's love and acceptance.* (In other words, the reward seems unattainable or unworthy of the cost.) *So I will run from the relationship through avoidance, obnoxiousness, explosive anger, self-deprecation, depression, or selfishness.*

How to Stir a Deadened Heart

The only way you can help your teenager fix these extreme fight-or-flight reactions to difficult relationships is both to teach and model for her a better way to respond to her pain. Your approach must be a do-as-I-say *and* do-as-I-do approach. So, if perfectionism, unmitigated conformity, isolation, and callousness are to be avoided, what should we be working to instill in the hearts of our teenagers? The attitudes and responses within the following principles will awaken their hearts:

- Principle 1: Because the need both to give and receive love and acceptance is inherently human, I will do everything in my power to obtain it for myself and provide it for others.
- Principle 2: Being loved and accepted as anyone other than who I really am is not true love and acceptance, so I will work to be authentically me all the time in my

relationships. This includes my personality, likes and dislikes, and feelings, but it also includes the boundaries I have set for myself and others.

- Principle 3: Though I will not pretend to be someone I'm not, I can choose at any moment to give to another person that part of myself she most needs. In turn, I give myself permission to ask others for that part of themselves that I need most. I do this, accepting ahead of time, that one or both of us may not be willing or able to give what is being asked for.

- Principle 4: I establish healthy relationships by striving to treat myself and others with the following attributes: love, joy, peace, patience, kindness, goodness, faithfulness, gentleness, and self-control.[1]

- Principle 5: I recognize that a deep relationship takes time. Therefore, I will be patient and not rush it by forcing myself on someone who is not ready to move deeper with me.

- Principle 6: If, as a result of my efforts, I find a healthy relationship, I will be thankful and appreciative, not taking it for granted but continually working to maintain it.

- Principle 7: If, despite my best efforts, I still lose the relationship, I will acknowledge my pain but not let it keep me from the hope of acceptance and love from someone else. To give up on the search for healthy relationships would be to give up on life itself.

I am fully aware that none of us is 100 percent successful at keeping these principles consistently all of the time, but the more mindful of them we are and the more we practice following them on a daily basis in our relationships, the stronger our hearts will be. The specifics of how to be a good friend, sibling, child, student, or significant other will come with time and experience. The goal is to keep your child from giving up and becoming complacent in the process. These principles will help her refocus on what's important and stay motivated to pursue people.

Restoring a Broken Heart

Modeling the attitudes above establishes a foundation on which your teenager can build healthy relationships, but you will also need to model actions that will help her navigate conflicts in her relationships. With each betrayal, rejection, or setback, she will want to come to you for help if—and only if—you have established a healthy method for walking her through her hurt. In this sense, the way you approach your teenager in the midst of her pain can be just as helpful as the actual advice you give. Here are some helpful tips:

Have an Open Invitation for Her to Vent Her Feelings

Be clear about this open invitation, then trust her to come to you so she doesn't accuse you of nagging, interfering, or prying into her business. She will know that when she is ready to talk, you will be there to listen. In this way, you will be modeling principles 3, 4, and 5 in your relationship with her. You cannot force your teenager to talk to you, but you can make it clear that you are ready and willing to help in times of crisis.

Listen, Listen, Listen

Once you've given the invitation and she takes you up on it, do just that: listen! Unfortunately, many teenagers feel betrayed when they share their hearts with their parents, because instead of listening, parents want to judge. Listening is an active process. If you have listened well, you should be able to communicate back to your child what she has told you and have her agree that that is exactly what she feels. It requires repetition, clarification, empathy, and reiteration.

Prejudice is the decision to formulate an opinion about the rightness or wrongness of someone's feelings without taking time to fully understand them. It is what we call jumping to a conclusion. If we do, we miss out on a vitally empowering part of the process of our teenagers' growth: being heard. More than anything, teenagers want to feel heard by others. What we do not realize is that this process also allows them to hear *themselves*. I am amazed at how often teenagers in my office will hear the absurdity or contradictions in their thoughts or feelings just by talking them out. Many times I do not have to say a word. A simple question like, "Is that what you really think?" causes them to pause and really think about it.

If we can provide this safe environment for our teenagers to process their thoughts and emotions, we can help them succeed in their other relationships by modeling principle 2. We also model for them what it is like to be a nonjudgmental listener for others.

Avoid the Quick Fix

Because we hate to see our kids in pain, it is easy to jump in and try to fix the problems in their relationships immediately.

This does several things: (1) it robs our kids of the responsibility of thinking for themselves, (2) makes them more dependent on us for the next problem they have, and/or (3) it may lead to feelings of anger and resentment toward us, the parents, when our solutions haven't worked out for them. Instead of the quick fix, collaborate with your teenager, let her take the driver's seat, and ride with her through the process. This becomes a give-and-take relationship that establishes principles 3, 4, 6, and 7. It also teaches your teenager that she neither has to be perfect nor has to conform to the pressures and demands placed on her by others.

Ask Permission to Give Advice

Sometimes we don't realize how empowering the simple gesture of granting us permission to give them advice can be for our kids. It communicates to them that we value their autonomy, their right of refusal, and their ability to choose. This gesture also frees us from being accused of manipulation, coercion, or rigidity, thus modeling principles 1 and 6. It also teaches our teenagers that in other relationships they do not have to be rigid, controlling, or opinionated to feel safe. We can allow others to think what they want while still maintaining our own beliefs.

Don't Be Offended by Pushback

As much as our children might want our opinions and as much as we might want to give them, we have to accept that they may choose different paths. If we let them do so, we communicate that success is within their power. If we refuse, we clearly communicate that they are not capable of succeeding. Also realize that some children are immediately defensive but come back around to our advice if we give them time. One of the keys of motivation is waiting until someone believes that the decision was her idea all along. She is much more likely to be motivated if she takes ownership of the decision. This is why it is absolutely essential that we do not get offended by pushback. This models principles 5 and 7, and it teaches our kids that disagreements in a relationship do not have to threaten the relationship.

Instill Belief in Her Ability to Figure It Out

Dependent teenagers usually remain so because they fear the responsibility of wrong choices. Parents also fear the consequences of the wrong choices our kids make. You can understand, then, why it might not be to your (or your child's) immediate advantage to allow for failure, but you must. When we believe in our kids, we are not denying that they will fail. We are accepting that they will grow from their failures and ultimately succeed. This is one of the greatest gifts we can give to them as they face struggles in their relationships.

Know Your Own Motives and Needs in Your Relationship with Your Teenager

This is the step that must permeate every other step on this list. Are you acting out of fear, anger, resentment, pride, or exhaustion? Do you want to avoid your teenager's rejection or secure her love? If you are not clear on this point, it may be helpful to talk to your spouse, a close adviser, or a professional therapist to get perspective. Most parents feel pressured by their kids to make quick decisions, but one of the most empowering statements you can make is, "Let me think about that." This models the alternative to the fight-or-flight reactions we see in our kids.

We wrongly assume that to be good parents, we should know the answers to our kids' problems immediately, but we are human just like our kids. When we tell our children we need to think about it, we are not communicating weakness so much as we are communicating intentionality, diligence, and the message that we take their needs, requests, thoughts, and emotions seriously. When in doubt, wait!

If you can practice these actions in the way you approach your teenager's relational problems, you will not only be more effective in helping her solve those problems, but you will be modeling for her the process of dealing with conflict in general. This will instill confidence in her to pursue people and will resurrect her undead heart.

Finding Models of a Healthy Heart

Zombie outbreaks spread quickly in areas where there are high concentrations of people. Like dominoes, people quickly succumb to and spread the infection that transforms living people into members of the undead.

There was a time when you had a great deal of control over who and what your child was exposed to. As she grow into a teenager, that control waned. More and more, your child's close proximity to others allows for the quick transmission of toxic and infectious ideas, attitudes, and behaviors that you never would have condoned. But it also allows for a testing of the waters, a way for your child to explore what a healthy, well-balanced relationship outside her family of origin looks like. The formative center of a teenager's relationships is shifting from the significance and love she receives as a member of your family to the significance and love she receives from her circle of friends, coaches, teachers, employers, and potential mates. You, as her parent, can challenge her to consider what kinds of relationships she has that are most fulfilling. While exploring this, challenge her to find models in her life who really do emulate the things she says she admires and wants.

Peer pressure is probably the single most destructive force to your child's identity and ability to engage in healthy relationships with others. To confront peer pressure, you need to talk explicitly with your teenager about who she is trying to be. Here we consider the types of people who impress your teenager. Her role models, if you will. Many people's role models have material possessions or accomplishments, such as money, fame, position, good looks, athleticism, and high IQs. There is nothing wrong with any of these things, but they shouldn't be the foundation on which we seek to emulate others. How people *use* their money, fame, position, looks, athleticism and intelligence is what makes them true role models.

Instead of focusing on people with material possessions and accomplishments to emulate, teenagers should focus on the people they admire for their relational qualities. "He is so friendly. She is so humorous. He is so driven. I like how caring he is, and I admire how giving she seems." These are the statements I cling to and explore further. These are examples of their "relational role models." What are the qualities and characteristics they see, consciously or unconsciously, in the people they admire? These are what should be brought to their attention and encouraged within them.

Avoiding the Infection of Your Own Heart

We've focused so far on helping teenagers deal with other relationships in their lives, but we as their parents are also human and susceptible to deadened hearts. We become discouraged and disheartened in our own relationships as much as our teenagers do in theirs. To be successful at awakening their hearts to others, we have to avoid overburdening them with our own personal relationship struggles. If this is happening, then we are the ones who have turned into zombies, feeding off of our children. Here are some pitfalls to avoid if you want to make your teenager as successful as possible in her relationships.

Feeding Off a Zombie's Vulnerability

In relationships there is a time and a place to be understood, but also a time and place to understand. We, as parents, set the precedent for this discernment. For example, let's pretend that your teenager felt ignored by a close friend at school today. You've been there before, right? But what if you are there right now? A coworker, church member, or trusted friend failed to return your call when you needed her most. You might be tempted to commiserate with your teenager, give vent to your own feelings of betrayal and rejection, and cling to your teenager in that moment of mutual understanding.

This is very dangerous. You've shifted the focus off of her need and onto your own. I've even seen parents go so far as to use their children's vulnerability to get back at them. They might say things like, "Well, now you know how I feel when you don't even say thank you for x, y, and z." Doing this may help you to feel known and heard in the moment, but not in the long run. In the future, your teenager will be inclined to avoid you when she is in pain because of your tendency to make it all about you. Avoid the immediate reward of having a listening ear for *your* troubles and focus on listening well to your teenager's struggles instead.

Befriending a Zombie

"My kids are also my friends. I love sharing with them, and we know each other so well. I don't see the problem with that!" If you don't, you will at some point! Friendship with our adult children isn't a bad thing. In fact, it's an appropriate relationship to hope for one day, but only after we have successfully launched our children into society. Sadly, many parents cling to the friendship they have with their teens and fail to encourage them to branch out toward others. If this continues, the teens' temporary failure to find dependability with people outside the family will lead them back to the safety and comfort of total dependency on their parents instead. Before the parents know it, they will find themselves in a toxically codependent relationship. No friendship, no matter how good, can survive this.

This symbiotic relationship between a parent and her zombie teenager is a unique bond. In order for undead children to remain complacent, self-centered, instantly gratified, and future-avoidant, they need the help of their parents. They latch on to the motivation, selflessness, strength, and planning of their parents like parasites feeding off the living. No wonder parents of undead adolescents feel like victims. The primary emotion for both parent and zombie, the one that perpetuates this vicious symbiotic relationship, is fear.

Later in the book, I will address the most common fears that keep parents stuck in this unhealthy relationship. The cycle can be broken, but the longer it has gone on, the more drastic the measures must be to break it.

Taking Self-Sacrifice Literally

Parents have a need to be needed. When we save our children from pain, we gain a sense of pride, accomplishment, and importance. Unfortunately, this mind-set can be taken to an extreme. You cannot help a zombie by letting it eat you alive! Our need to be needed can interfere with our ability to empower our kids to face life's challenges on their own.

You do not always have to pay for traffic tickets, e-mail teachers to obtain extensions on homework, change plans to accommodate your child's failure to be ready on time, make special meals to cater to her picky appetite, or let her control the television or play video games all weekend. Of course, any one of these actions in isolation may be appropriate in a specific circumstance, but making them the norm is not saving your teenage zombie. It is simply feeding your need to be needed.

Chaining a Zombie

Instead of allowing for their children's unique identities, parents sometimes try to create mini-me versions of themselves so they can effectively manage the judgments others make about their teenagers and themselves as parents. In doing so, they fail to respect the budding autonomy of their teenagers.

For example, I know many teenage clients who turn away from their parents' belief systems, not because the beliefs is unreasonable but because the parents' enforcement of the beliefs was unreasonable. The teens have not been given the choice to adopt the belief as their own. You can imagine how suffocating this might be to a teenager who desperately wants to become her own person.

Do not hide behind your teenager. Accept that there will be times when she will honor you and times when she will disappoint you. You must allow for both if your goal is to resurrect a zombie! She must have an identity apart from you in order to have a healthy relationship with you.

Failing to Set an Emotional Perimeter

Emotions fluctuate from moment to moment and can be influenced by many factors unrelated to your child's behavior. If you allow your emotions to dictate your approval or disapproval of your child, she will be very confused about how to succeed as your child, and she will carry that confusion into other relationships too.

For example, if you are in a silly mood and you let your child's disrespectful sarcastic comments slide, but you demand that she speak respectfully when you are in a bad mood, you are sending mixed signals. You are telling her that she must tiptoe around your feelings, which are unpredictable and inconsistent. Because kids have a tendency to test the limits of what we will tolerate to see where the boundaries are, this inconsistency will lead your teenager to defy you in open rebellion or to retreat into helplessness. She will have no idea what the boundaries are, let alone develop an ability to maintain them.

Emotional boundaries are just as important as the material and circumstantial boundaries we set for maintaining order in the home. Many parents at this stage of their child's development have tried and failed over and over again to set material and circumstantial boundaries—the rules, requirements, and responsibilities we assign our kids so that they may gain privileges and material/financial rewards in the home. These material and circumstantial boundaries can be explicitly developed in the form of a behavioral contract, but the contracts are useless if parents do not maintain the emotional control necessary to enforce them. Teenagers have an uncanny knack for playing on our emotions like an electric guitar. You can go through all the work of creating contracts, setting rules, and outlining consequences and rewards, but if you cannot handle your own emotions, all that work will be useless.

This is where working with your spouse helps. You can vent your frustration, sadness, anger, or resentment to your spouse behind closed doors, regroup, and then face your teenager in a calm way after the emotional storm has died down. If you are a single parent, I recommend relying on a close friend or mentor with whom you can share your struggles. Learn to demonstrate consistency in the expression of your controlled emotions so that your child knows what pleases you and what does not. She will not only develop confidence in her ability to navigate her relationship with you, but she will also seek out relationships that provide that same kind of stability and consistency, avoiding other volatile people who might destroy her.

Now that we have addressed the challenges of having a zombie brain and heart, it is time to consider the zombie spirit. As you will see in the next section, the zombie spirit has been broken. Here is where we must step in and bring clarity to the importance of an overall philosophy of life that teenagers can take with them into a very scary world filled with other zombies.

Strategy Questions

1. Do you see patterns developing in your teenager's attitude and actions when dealing with difficulties in his or her relationships? What are the difficulties and what are the typical reactions you see? Be as specific as possible.

2. The seven principles for healthy boundaries in our relationships, which are listed in this chapter, are written with a formal tone. What can you do this week to begin passing them on—teaching and modeling them—to your teenager in ways he or she can understand and emulate? Be specific to the problem relationships your child is facing right now.

CHAPTER 5

The Teenage Zombie Spirit

To resurrect your undead adolescent, you have to understand what you are resurrecting him to. This is the plight of the undead: they do not know what real life is. If adolescents have faulty expectations of what life is supposed to be like, then their disillusionment will eventually rob them of the joy life affords.

Brian, the young man whose story I opened this book with, was a perfect example of a teenager who'd lost an understanding of what real life is. What caused Brian to try drugs in the first place? Aside from a genetic predisposition to addictive behaviors, something that should not be ignored, there are a number of other psychological factors that drove him to use. He felt the pressure from his peers and wanted to be liked. He was bored and wanted to experience a thrill. He was dealing with the stress of school and needed some relief. In addition, he was unknowingly medicating an underlying depression. There was even an aspect of rebellion against the constraints of his parents and society, whom he felt had hurt him in the past.

In all of these motivating factors, the key feature to Brian's initial use was a faulty perspective on the reality of life and how to live it. In this section, I will focus on three truths about life every zombie must know if he wishes to avoid the zombified state I witnessed in Brian in the hospital.

Life Is a Process, Not an End Point

Zombie flicks are essentially life-and-death struggles. Likewise, every teen wants to know, "Can I survive this world I'm living in?" But, like all people, teenagers don't just want to survive; they want to experience life to the fullest. They fear they might "miss out" on all that life has to offer, but if they tell themselves that they will be truly alive at some point in the future, they miss out on the life there is to live right now.

When an adolescent sits down in my office and says, "I feel dead inside," they are really telling me, "I am struggling to live in the moment. The life I have now doesn't seem to be enough." Parents find it extremely confusing to hear their children question the quality of their lives, especially when they have done so much to help them experience life to the fullest. Why can't they be satisfied with what they have? Usually it is because they are viewing life as an end point to be achieved rather than a process to experience.

If we are honest with ourselves, we make the same mistake. We anticipated that life would start when we found our soul mate, when we finished school, when we got our first job, when we had our first child. Now we believe life only happens on the weekends, when we've purchased that dream home, or when we've gotten the promotion we've been hoping for. We will be proud of our children when they graduate, when they get married, when they get their first job, or when they have their first child.

This is a deadening perspective. To escape the deadness of life, we must work to be present in the moment, engaging our minds fully in the tasks, relationships, thoughts, emotions, and bodily sensations that permeate our existence at any given time. This is challenging, especially given all the devices and activities that allow us to escape mentally, even when we may be present bodily. It is doable, however, if we practice mindfulness in the moment, accept the process of living, and loosen our grip on a preconceived end point to our existence.

This truth is vital for your teenager to understand. There is no moment in time when he will suddenly say, "Ah, now I've arrived. This is real living." Unfortunately, society pounds that message into teenagers every day. Advertisers give different solutions for finding meaning, pleasure, and fulfillment in life. Each one claims to have a cure-all that will provide protection against the zombie-like deadness that threatens to leave your child in a meaningless, pleasureless existence. "You'd better get it now," they say, "or you will be left behind." The fixes these advertisers offer will not last, and they know it. They want your teenager coming back for more. That's what keeps them in business. So they must continue to propagate the idea that real life is waiting just around the corner.

Your teenager does not have to be deceived. Life is already ours. It is in the sips of coffee we take first thing in the morning as we get ready for the day. It is in the warmth of the sun or the chill of the rain we feel on our shoulders as we walk from the front door to our car. It is in the words we say to one another when there is really nothing to talk about. It is in the struggle of studying long hours for an exam or staying up late to finish a project for work. It is in a smile, a touch, a tear, a connection—no matter how brief. The key to life is awareness of it, observing it as it permeates us. Whether high or low or somewhere in between, life is a constant ebb and flow, a process we have no choice but to participate in. To be conscious participants or unconscious participants: that is really the only choice we have.

Please understand that I am not advocating a live-*for*-the-moment mind-set in which people make decisions based solely on what makes them happy right now. What I am advocating is a live-*in*-the-moment mind-set that allows you to face each challenge and triumph as it comes without the dissatisfaction and disillusionment that happen when we get too far ahead of ourselves. This leads us to the second truth about life that teenagers have to accept.

Life Has Limits

The adolescent years are usually the first time we confront one important truth about life: as finite beings, there is only so much "life" we can handle. If you can communicate this effectively to your teenager, you will save him from many problems. You will rid him of the sense that he is missing out on something big, something that is going to satisfy his deepest needs at very little or no cost to himself.

There is an ancient prayer that says roughly, "God don't make me too wealthy or too poor. If I am too wealthy, I might forget you or believe I don't need you. If I am too poor, I might steal from someone else and dishonor your name."[1] Balance is the key to a full life. This balance includes a healthy perspective on money, material pleasures, relationships, time, and personal goals. It involves all elements of life biologically, psychologically, socially, and spiritually. A zombie devours anything and everything in its path without ever being satisfied. Consequently, everything a teenage zombie does is destructive to himself and to others. Fail to communicate to your teenager that pleasure has limits, and you will find yourself being devoured by his voracious, unquenchable appetite. Teach him the limits of what the material world can offer him, and you will save his life.

Use the metaphor of a pole or cap when it comes to pleasure and pain. As we move toward a northern cap of pleasure, we reach a pole at which continued movement forward changes our direction south, toward pain. This is true of every aspect of life. A gentle massage can feel good for a while but becomes irritating if it lasts too long.[2] Consider how we long for the changing of seasons, routines, and scenery. Try listening to your favorite song a hundred times over and see if it is still your favorite song by the end of the day. Eat the same meal three times a day for a month and see if you still enjoy it as much as you did.

All beauty fades with the progression of time, leaving us wanting something new, fresh, and undiscovered. That's why we say variety is the spice of life, but if we have too much variety, we long for consistency, stability, and the familiar. Medications given to relieve suffering can potentially trigger addiction and other long-term health problems. Ironically, dopamine, the substance understood to be the chemical basis of all that is joyful, rewarding, and pleasurable about life, is stimulated in our brains by dangerous substances, one of which is literally called the "zombie drug." This drug causes dopamine to be trapped inside the brain at toxic levels, creating an experience that is unintended by the user, one of unfathomable pain, fear, and even brain-death.[3] It is too much of a good thing.

Relationally, these limits also exist. The law of diminishing returns states that for any given investment of energy, there is a point at which the benefits become less than the effort expended. When we consider how desperately one needs and how aggressively one pursues love and belonging, there is a point at which one's efforts become toxic to the relationship. C. S. Lewis likened the intensity we feel in these kinds of relationships to a man ravenous with thirst who consumes delicious drinks with indifference to the quality of the drinks.[4] Sometimes we cannot appreciate the quality of our relationships because of how desperately we need them. The needier we are in our relationships, the more aware we are of the other's deficiencies and failure to meet our needs.

When your teenager recognizes these limitations, begins to live in the moment, and enjoys the process of life instead of looking to an imaginary end point, he or she develops a key component that is needed for resurrection into a meaningful, fulfilling life: contentment.

Contentment is a tenant for tranquility in almost every religious and spiritual group throughout history. Without it, we will always be miserable. Most people, however, view contentment as an end point in the future or a goal to achieve once an identified set of requirements is met. This is an incorrect view of contentment. Contentment is a state of mind, not a function of our circumstances. Your teenager needs contentment as he begins making choices for the future. You need contentment as you struggle to raise your teen.

"But I'm not content! I don't accept my teenager's laziness, lack of motivation, drug and alcohol use, failing grades, mischievous friends. How can you tell me to be content with these things?" I understand your objections. Contentment is not com-placency. You should not accept these as static, lasting traits or behaviors in your teenager, but you must accept the reality of them at present, even as you work toward change. Otherwise, you might end up making things worse.

I remind my clients that there are times in life when we must be comfortable with the uncomfortable. It is the only way to stay calm, think rationally, and make healthy choices for the good of everyone involved. If you cannot be content with uncomfortable situations, you are likely to make rash decisions to escape quickly. In doing so, you might find immediate relief from pain, but it will not be a lasting, healthy, or helpful escape in the long run.

For example, I know an adolescent named Jessica who was failing her classes. She was focused on cheerleading and social-izing with her friends and was not taking her education seriously. Her dad could not accept this, so he took action. He contacted all of Jessica's teachers, made excuses for her, and asked them to accommodate, make exceptions, and increase her one-on-one tutoring time. This worked for a time, but his daughter got used to the special attention, leniency, and exceptions, and her efforts declined even further. When her grades slipped again, her father, again unable to accept her failure, lost his temper. He began to reprimand her, accusing her of being ungrateful and blaming her for the rising tension in their home, all this while hiring professional tutors on top of the special attention she was receiving at school. He began pouring more money into the problem while resenting his daughter even more.

Of course, you know what happened: nothing. The grades did not improve, but now there grew a rift between father and daughter. Instead of gratitude, Jessica felt hatred toward her father, seeing his efforts as evidence that he was ashamed of her as a person. What happened here? Jessica's father was not content to allow his daughter to fail. The possibility of her repeating a grade was not acceptable to him; therefore, he was willing to do anything to prevent it. Much of his frantic effort centered on his own embarrassment at having to acknowledge the failure to other families in their social circle. As a result, he found himself doing more work than his daughter was willing to do in order to achieve a preconceived notion of success. Ultimately, his actions were destructive in the end. If Jessica's father had been content with the possibility of her failure, he may have been able to take a step back, talk it through with Jessica, and develop a plan of action that involved her more. Instead, he was taken down by a teenage zombie. Keep this story in mind as you continue reading.

Life Has a Definite Purpose

Most of us, even those of us who have coddled suicidal thoughts, would acknowledge that deep down we want to live. But the answer to "why" can be challenging. A form of deadness takes over when we realize that almost everything about life fails to satisfy us completely. In a strange, almost maddening irony, the more aggressively we pursue life apart from a clear metaphysical or spiritual worldview, we find ourselves in a deeper state of deadness than we previously thought possible.

Step back for a moment and remember what it was like to be a teenager on the verge of leaving home. Imagine standing at the brink of a new life, one where you are now ultimately responsible for the direction you take. Think about all those deep questions you had at the time. "What should I be when I grow up? How can I make a difference in the world? Who will I commit my life to? Will I be happy? Will I succeed?" Some of us have forgotten these questions because we've gotten comfortable with the routine. We are used to the subtler ebbs and flows of day-to-day life and are rarely confronted with the extreme highs we dreamed of or the extreme lows we dreaded when we were young. We are just going through the motions.

The challenge in raising teenagers is that we must wrestle with these issues all over again. Many parents who are facing challenges with their teenagers are dealing with their own midlife crises at the same time. While your teenager is asking, "What am I going to do?" you may be asking, "What have I been doing?" While your teenager is asking, "Who am I going to become," you may be asking, "What have I become?"

The ultimate question both you and your teenager are asking is "Why live?" This is what we call an "existential question." It is metaphysical, or beyond what can be answered by the scientific method. It is the challenge of defining our purpose for being alive. What makes the pain worth enduring or the pleasure worth enjoying? There is no exact formula or questionnaire we can complete to help us answer it, but it is the most important question we ask as we go through life: What is the point?

The point of our immediate existence often changes. We need to study hard so that we can get accepted to college. We need to work hard to earn money to pay bills. We need to exercise to stay healthy. We find someone to marry so that we can feel loved. These are all purposes that help to define why we do what we do in the moment, but we also need long-term goals, dreams, and aspirations. Some people live solely to experience pleasure. They "live for the weekend," so to speak. Others live to serve people and feel significant by how they touch the lives of others. Some people enjoy creating things. Others enjoy exploration and discovery. Some enjoy pushing themselves to the limits of their abilities. Some believe that their purpose is to please and honor God in whatever they choose to do. They adhere to a religious system that helps them gauge how successful they are in fulfilling that purpose.

Whatever your overarching philosophy about life is, you must be conscious of it and you must challenge your teenager to be conscious of his. This ultimate purpose instilled within him will be the driving force that keeps him alive and out of the undead, zombified state you fear for him.

In addition to knowing your purpose in life, it is also important to understand that crises will challenge that purpose. These crises are inevitable and must be answered and endured. Philosophers have narrowed these crises down to four major struggles. What is interesting is that they are always the major themes addressed in every Zombie flick, embedded deep beneath the violence and gore depicted on the screen. Understanding these struggles will explain why the undead archetype (or metaphor) evokes dread in the hearts and minds of, not only children, but also adults. They also explain why pop culture keeps us tantalized with the subject matter.

Death, the first existential crisis, is not some future event but a constant reality in our lives. Irvin D. Yalom, a famous psychiatrist and author, described death as "whirring softly, barely audibly, just under the membrane of consciousness."[5] In zombie movies, the characters are always faced with death. The question we ask in the face of death is, "What am I doing right now of importance, and will it have value after I am gone?"

Isolation, the second existential crisis, is felt by many teenagers who, though more connected to their peers through advances in technology, still struggle with loneliness, deadened by the virtual nature of their interactions. In zombie movies, the characters are always isolated and surrounded by the zombies, struggling to make connection with the outside world before they are consumed. The question we ask when faced with the crisis of isolation is, "What am I doing to foster love and belonging in my relationships?"

Meaninglessness is another existential crisis depicted by the zombies' mindless wandering and destructive devouring of the living. It raises fear in the hearts of teenagers who question the relevance of their own existence in a looming world of responsibilities and daily demands. The question we ask when faced with the crisis of meaningless is, "What are the rewards for my actions, and are they enough to sustain my continued efforts in this situation?"

Finally, freedom, from an existentialist's point of view, is not a privilege or right, but a burden, one that teenagers begin to question in the face of society's collapsing morals and traditions. In zombie movies, governmental controls and societal norms are broken in the chaos, and individuals bear the complete weight of responsibility in deciding actions that lead either to their survival or demise. When faced with the crisis of freedom, we are left asking, "Is there is any redemption in the face of my failure to choose wisely? And is there a greater plan, order, or control that will absolve me?"

These are the battles of the mind that your teenager is just beginning to fight, but they may also be ones you have fought for years. How you answer these questions will determine how you fight the deadness in your own life and how you teach your child to fight it in his life also. Success requires the acceptance of and contentment with life as a process with very clear limits and a well-defined ultimate purpose that guides your teenager through pleasure and pain alike. Sound impossible? It is not. Don't give up on yourself or your teenager.

Strategy Questions

1. What is your overarching philosophy about the following issues?
    a. the cycle of life and death
    b. the purpose of and meaning behind life
    c. the point of relationships and community
    d. the balance of freedom and responsibility

2. If there was one truth for each of these questions that you would like for your teenager to understand and accept, what would it be?

PART 2

Facing Our Fear
of Zombies

CHAPTER 6

The Fear of Deception

The undead have haunted the dreams of children and adults for centuries. Novels like *Frankenstein* and *Dracula* are classics, required reading for most educational curriculums. Undead lore is particularly titillating because it preys on several elemental fears most cultures have. These same fears parallel the anxieties that parents have when dealing with their zombie teenagers. These fears are what keep parents and children stuck in the psychological feeding frenzy that tears individuals and families apart.

Zombie movies, like other horror films, are scary primarily because of the deception involved. Most victims are taken by surprise. In the same way, nearly all parents have fears that their children may be pulling a fast one on them. It is not unusual for a parent to freak out when a child is caught sneaking out after curfew, watching pornography, gaming in the middle of the night, smoking or drinking alcohol for the first time, or experimenting sexually. Parents can also be caught off guard by other less dramatic surprises: the first time a child questions the logic behind household rules, challenges the family's religious beliefs or practices, or breaks family traditions by pursuing a particular career or relationship. Parents who are not aware of the natural progression of the adolescent stage of development are surprised by this seemingly sudden transformation in their children's behavior. They have different hobbies, musical tastes, and opinions on clothing, politics, and social activities. They challenge the rules that had previously been accepted as law. Some begin to experiment with lifestyle choices that you, the parents, know are wrong. When we feel caught off guard by these challenges to our authority and wisdom, it is easy for us to kick into a fight-or-flight mode of reacting. Everything we knew and understood to be right for ourselves and our kids is being attacked. Although it isn't pleasant, it is common, even normal, for adolescents who once conformed to our standards to now challenge and defy them.

In this way, your adolescent is like a zombie. A zombie starts out as a normal human being but gets infected, usually from the bite of another zombie. Your teenage zombie knows your expectations. Her curiosity lies in understanding the rules and expectations of her expanding peer group, society, and culture. She begins to make decisions based on these new spheres of influence. Once this transformation begins, a zombie still has some resemblance to the human it once was.

Our shock and horror as parents occurs when we approach a zombie, thinking it is a human being like us, only to realize that we have been *deceived* by the humanlike qualities of the undead. Before we know it, the zombie is upon us, tearing us apart. No one ever knows when she might inadvertently stumble upon a zombie. If we fall for the deception and live to tell about it, we may find it difficult to shake the sense of vulnerability that has risen inside of us. We find it hard to trust again: trust the person that attacked us or trust our own assessment of future situations. We no longer take anything for granted. We find ourselves always on the defensive, emotionally and physically exhausted. We've been unnerved!

Stephanie, the single mom of a fifteen-year-old son named Jordan, admitted that when she walked in on her son viewing pornography one evening, she exploded. In her anger, she lashed out at him, accused him of being a sex addict, and then could hardly look at him for the next week. She thought of all kinds of ways to punish Jordan for his betrayal: she could take his computer away for life, send him to a therapeutic boarding school, maybe even check him into a monastery! Instead, she just refused to speak to him beyond the perfunctory exchanges necessary to complete day-to-day tasks. The point is, Stephanie freaked out.

Stephanie later reflected that her attitude and actions toward Jordan were wrong, but she was so taken aback by her son's behavior, she could not control herself. She never thought that he was "that kind of kid." Stephanie had worked hard to raise her two sons to respect women. This was especially important to her because she had been abused as a teenager by an older man. Her son's behavior brought back all the hurt and shame of her past, and she reacted out of fear. She felt deceived by the son she thought she knew. Unfortunately, she wasn't able to take back the words she had spoken in anger toward Jordan, but she was able to make amends with him, ask his forgiveness, and find a male mentor through Jordan's guidance counselor at school. This man took Jordan under his wing, encouraging and challenging him in ways that Stephanie could not.

Caught Off Guard

It is important to note that Stephanie's fear and protective response toward her son's unexpected actions is a normal reaction for all of us. When we become aware of a deception, whether it is someone's intentional attempt to hide something from us or our own failure to recognize the reality of a situation, we feel threatened.

This is a common occurrence in the animal kingdom. Many animals use deception as a means to repel a predator or to attract prey. The deception provides a way of escape or control. If another animal falls for the deception, it either goes without lunch or becomes lunch. It is natural for our fight-or-flight responses to surge through our brains and bodies when we are caught off guard by our children's actions.

Some deceptions are our fault. Our teenagers were not intentionally trying to deceive us. We were just caught off guard by their natural behaviors. However, teenagers will intentionally use deception in similar ways to predators and prey: to escape conflict, avoid punishment, protect their privacy, or take control. Some level of privacy and experimentation is important for developing adolescents. They need a chance to formulate their own ideas and learn from their experiences. Parents have to find the balance between two very important jobs of parenting adolescents: (1) the need to invade a teenager's privacy in order to protect them, and (2) the need to gradually relinquish control of their children's decisions in order to foster their independence. A healthy fear of deception keeps us intentionally involved in our children's lives, but it also allows us to remain calm, cool, and collected when it is time to intervene. If we can anticipate danger, we are more likely to be prepared for it.

Making Use of Deception

Being intentional about helping our teenagers transition through adolescence should include an ongoing and open dialogue about their thoughts, emotions, and upcoming decisions on a day-to-day basis. This dialogue should also include a gracious but firm reiteration of our expectations and hopes for our teens.

Now, dialogue is great, but we all know how difficult it can be to engage a teenage zombie in a forced conversation. It can feel like Tom Hanks talking to a volleyball. "Hey, Wilson, there is a storm coming. What do you think we should do? . . . Yeah, that's what I thought!"

This is where a healthy dose of "deception" on your part can actually serve you well. What do I mean by *deception* here? I mean creating environments and experiences with your teenager where your agenda is not so blatantly obvious. Think about it: as an adult, do *you* like to be lectured? Of course not. The same is true for teenagers. They are moving into adulthood, wanting to make their own decisions and feel more in control of their lives. If parents do not see this change taking place, they walk right into the trap of teenage angst, defensiveness, cynicism, and defiance by confronting problems aggressively out of anger and fear as they arise. When we are acting intentionally in our kids' lives, however, we can do two things to reduce the frequency and severity of these conflicts: (1) we can observe the changes taking place within our teenagers without directly engaging them, and then (2) we can create environments that foster natural conversations about these changes. If these natural encounters are occurring on a regular basis, we do not have to be as stressed when we don't get to every issue of concern immediately. We can allow things to unfold naturally, rather than feeling blindsided by a sudden crisis issue that we must fix immediately.

As I was growing up, these natural exchanges of information sometimes occurred around family meals. I had three siblings and we were all given the opportunity to speak about our days, problems we were having, and questions we had about life. We were not forced to speak if we didn't want to, but we all had the chance to listen. Through storytelling, problem-solving, and sometimes downright silliness, we had the chance to learn from and experience one another in a natural way. This scheduled time for connecting was absolutely important. However, it was more of a time for us to learn that our parents wanted us to bring our problems, questions, and good news to them. This established the foundation, but some of the most meaningful talks occurred during unplanned encounters: driving to a game or the local ice cream place, working on a project together, tossing the football, or watching a movie. Mom and Dad were used to being interrupted, but if they couldn't talk then, they would say so and plan to meet with us at a later time. One of the biggest helps was their willingness to be open about their own struggles and how they dealt with them. As a result of years of intentional engagement, I knew that Mom and Dad were always available to talk and listen when necessary. I also witnessed their relative calm when dealing with major problems that arose.

Of course, there were definitely times in our home when direct confrontation over specific problems was necessary, but because Mom and Dad knew each of us so well, more often than not they reacted with calm, rational responses to our behaviors.

Fighting and Flighting

The danger of being deceived or caught off guard by a zombie teenager lies in the extreme emotional reactions that can govern our decisions in those moments: rigid control that stifles and demoralizes teenagers or a head-in-the-sand attitude that ignores potential dangers and puts children's physical, psychological, and spiritual well-being at risk.

These extreme reactions are usually based in a desire to protect a parent's own psychological well-being. We will discuss these threats to our psychology more as we explore each of the subsequent fears associated with zombie teenagers, but they include our need to maintain our reputation, our dignity, and our sense of significance, peace, security, comfort, and control, just to name a few. When these are threatened, we act impulsively and emotionally to maintain the equilibrium of the established system in the home. Controlling (fight) or escaping (flight) are the quickest ways to squelch our fears. To control, we shout, accuse, threaten, name-call, or at worst become physically aggressive. But there are passive forms of aggression too: making comparisons to other siblings, giving our kids the silent treatment, or denying or withdrawing our feelings to punish or confuse. To escape, we ignore the problem, rationalize it away, make excuses, pass the buck, distract ourselves with other pursuits like hobbies or work, or at worst, numb them with drugs, alcohol, food, and sex.

Immediate reactions make us feel better in the short term, but in the long term, they don't address the problem. We still have a zombie in the house and we find ourselves in danger of becoming one ourselves. Parents who stay somewhere in the middle of controlling and escaping must wrestle with the tension of an uncomfortable situation. They are forced to find the difficult balance between caring for their own needs and the needs of their kids. Each decision must be thought out with diligence and care, but these parents are usually rewarded for their perseverance in the long run.

Tolerating the Threat

Sitting with discomfort is very challenging, even biologically. With my clients, I liken the stressful feelings we experience when watching a horror movie. The first time you watch it, you want to run out of the theater or keep your eyes closed the whole time. The second time you watch it, the movie isn't as scary because you can predict what is going to happen. The third, fourth, and fifth times you watch it, you feel bored. The more we are confronted with these situations and the more we wrestle with them, the more power we have to act calmly, rationally, and intentionally. Nevertheless, this is easier said than done.

Did you know that scientists have actually taken time to study how the brain reacts to situations that catch us off guard? To do this, they studied the disturbing sensations we feel when confronted with something that is "almost human but not." Think about the source material for thousands of horror films: clowns, mimes, robots, dolls, and animals that have eerily human qualities but are wholly other than human. Why do they scare us? Because our brains are being tricked by features that we recognize on entities that are not like anything we've seen before.

Functional MRIs performed on individuals observing these almost-human beings demonstrated significant changes of signaling in the parietal lobes of the brain.

Unfortunately, our brains can be tricked by similarities in situations that are actually very different. Imagine walking through the woods and reaching down to pick up a walking stick, only to realize it is actually a snake! When the brain realizes it has been tricked, it reacts impulsively, preparing the body for the threat behind the deception. Our heart rate increases, our eyes dilate, our skin prickles with goose bumps, and our stomach turns. *How could I have been deceived?* we wonder. We feel betrayed, spooked. This same reaction occurs when we experience something that looks human but really isn't. Guess what image scientists found most likely to generate this sudden physiological response in subjects participating in the study? You guessed it: zombies.[1]

Imagine what happens when your expectations of reality are challenged by your zombie teenager's actions. Jack was like any father of a teenage daughter: protective. Whenever boys would come to the house or call to talk to his daughter, Amanda, he would embarrass her by grilling them with questions and making subtle threats of bodily harm if they ever took advantage of her. Jack didn't want Amanda to settle for just any guy. In fact, with her intelligence, he hoped that she would follow in his footsteps and go to medical school. Imagine his horror when he discovered in the early morning hours of homecoming weekend that his daughter had gotten drunk at a party and posted some risqué pictures to her Facebook account. He was livid.

Fortunately for everyone involved, Jack unleashed all of his fury, fear, and freaking out in the presence of his wife, Carolyn, before Amanda got home. Carolyn talked him through his anxieties, helped him to see that things could have been a lot worse, and processed an appropriate punishment for Amanda with him. By the time Amanda arrived home, Jack had calmed down.

He avoided exploding and instead first expressed his love and thankfulness that she was okay. With that clearly stated, he and Carolyn allowed Amanda to get some sleep. The next morning they discussed her punishment, its rationale, and their concerns and expectations for her future decisions.

Jack could have blown it that morning if he had reacted rashly. If he had freaked out when Amanda returned, he could have said things he would have regretted. Amanda already felt a great deal of shame over her actions. She was embarrassed and afraid. Her father's gentleness in response helped her to see that he still believed in her, thought no less of her, and still wanted what was best for her. Because of this, she accepted her punishment more willingly: one month without use of the car on weekends, no more unsupervised parties, and six months of weekly volunteer work at the downtown homeless shelter.

Let's face it. Not all situations work out as neatly as Jack's. We blow it often. The best advice I can give is to be willing to own your failures with your kids and apologize. Failures do not undermine your authority. Stubbornness and defensiveness do. Embracing your humanity is a surefire way to avoid becoming a zombie.

Rebuilding Trust after a Scare

There are psychological ramifications of falling for a teenage zombie's deception or being caught off guard by unforeseen problems. If our notion of what is true in the world is proven wrong, we can lose our confidence to move forward. We feel confused and paralyzed. Many parents of undead adolescents arrive at therapists' offices in a panic. They are looking for help to explain their children's actions. They need solutions to fix the problems they either did not see coming or had underestimated. Many are dumbfounded by the actions of their children, which are so contrary to their standards. "After all we have done for our children, how could they turn around and betray us like this?" The parents' trust has been broken and it will take time for the teens to regain it. Here are some important tips to keep in mind as you work to rebuild that trust:

Hope for the Best, Prepare for the Worst

There may be a perfect family out there somewhere, but yours is not. Neither is mine. Be prepared for anything. It is important that you anticipate the challenges your budding zombie is in danger of confronting. Read books on adolescent development to become informed in a general sense. Be involved at your daughter's school; know her teachers, her friends, her friends' parents, and the activities she is involved in. Make your home a place where your teen and her friends want to hang out. Talk to her early about sex, alcohol, drugs, video games, and schoolwork. Keep your eyes open for potential learning disabilities, anxieties, or social stressors that might discourage your child and lead her to make poor choices. Process with your spouse, close family member, or friend ahead of time how you will deal with certain scenarios should they to arise.

Stay Calm

Losing your temper or freaking out will not solve the problem. It can only make it worse. Realize that your extreme emotional reactions usually come from psychological stressors that you have not dealt with effectively. Maybe you have a stressful job or conflict in other relationships. Maybe you are placing too much of your significance on the outcome of your children's lives. Maybe you have an anger or anxiety disorder that could be helped through psychotherapy or medication. We all blow it at times, but if you have a pattern of exacerbating stressors in the home, it may be time to focus inward before you try to fix your zombie teenager.

Remember: losing your cool does the opposite of what you are trying to accomplish. When you explode in anger or anxiety, you are telling your kids that you cannot be trusted, that your decisions are just as impulsive as theirs, and that you are less concerned about their well-being and more concerned about your psychological and emotional needs. I cannot stress enough that you must process these needs in other contexts: with your spouse, your therapist, your close friends, and family. Parents are the stable framework that help a teenager grow into a strong and mature adult. Be that stable and predictable framework for your kids.

Seek Understanding

One thing we learn as therapists: if your clients do not feel as if you understand them, they will not listen to what you have to say. Help your budding adolescent know that you are always there for her. Explain the reasons behind rules in the household. If at all possible, be known as a parent who loves to say yes but says no for good reasons. As your adolescent changes, be curious about the person she is becoming. Ask questions. Show a genuine interest in her tastes, interests, and ideas. The more you understand her, the more you will be able to help her, and the more she will be willing to listen to you as well. Everyone has a need to be known and understood. Part of understanding your teenager is understanding in general why she tends to be so impulsive and emotional. Until then, recognize that your child may not always understand her behavior. Simply being understanding of her lack of understanding is extremely powerful in developing that level of trust you will need to positively influence her life.

When you know there is going to be a zombie attack, you can stockpile your guns, ammo, and canned goods so that you will be prepared for the onslaught. The same is true for dealing with the deceptive, unpredictable, and frightening experiences of raising zombie teenagers. Be prepared. Do your homework. Stay calm and zombie on. The best thing you can do as a parent of a zombie teenager is to be an intentional presence in her life. Realize that teenagers can be scary and unpredictable, but with intentionality, diligence, and genuine care, you can successfully bring them through and have a lot of fun in the process. That is something not to be deceived about.

Strategy Questions

1. What are the major struggles in your teenager's life that you may be turning a blind eye toward? What specifically can you do to be more conscious of these issues and how they are affecting your teenager on a daily basis?

2. Given your personality, what are some specific strategies you can employ to avoid reacting too quickly and too intensely to those situations in your teenager's life that take you by surprise?

CHAPTER 7

The Fear of Association

No one wants to be associated with a zombie. Take a moment and consider the attributes of the fictional undead. Zombies symbolize the absolute worst aspects of humanity. They look like humans but are repulsive in form. They have some mannerisms similar to humans, but their actions are only self-gratifying and destructive. They appear to have feelings (mainly rage), but they are unable to reflect on those feelings or temper them in the same way humans do. Zombies have some capacity to think, but they are incapable of considering the thoughts or feelings of others. Unfortunately, many of these attributes may sound like our kids at times. What's worse, they may sound like us!

Now consider the human characters in all zombie stories. At first, you might say that the zombies are the antagonists and the humans are the protagonists, but that is not true. Typically, the protagonists and antagonists are both humans, faced with a moral decision or dilemma that will determine their fate. By juxtaposing two human characters who are at odds, writers of undead fiction force us to confront the question, "If I were in this situation, would I make the right decision? Would I be a hero or a villain?" The zombies are a threat, certainly, but survival is always dependent on the decisions of the *human* characters in the stories, good and bad.

Once these decisions are made, the living have a chance to reflect on their decisions through face-to-face encounters with the undead. Sometimes the living feel guilty. They see someone like themselves whom they could have saved. Now the zombie before them is a shell of its former self.

Mirror, Mirror on the Xbox

These same kinds of encounters occur almost daily for parents of zombie teenagers. Just as zombies are a reflection of the worst aspects of humanity, our zombie teenagers can reflect back on us the worst aspects of ourselves: our anger, obstinacy, pride, and selfishness. We are never more aware of our own flaws and shortcomings as when we are dealing with the failures of our kids. Like Dr. Frankenstein, we look at the creation before us, the one glued to the Xbox, and cry out, "What have I done?"

It is normal, when things go wrong, to want to ascribe blame where it is due. One reason we do this is that human brains are wired to think in terms of cause and effect. This process allows us to make sense of the world and use that knowledge to make choices based on predictable outcomes. As a baby, we learn that if we cry, our mothers will feed us. As toddlers, we learn that if we touch a hot stove, we will get burned. As elementary school students, we learn that we I color within the lines, our teachers will give us a sticker. Notice that with each one of these internalized experiences, our brains develop rules for how to think and act to achieve the desired outcome.

Problems arise, however, when our brains try to make sense of unexplainable, unachieved, or unexpected outcomes. We feel uncomfortable with things that do not make sense, so we assign blame. It is our brains' normal reaction to situations we believe must have a cause-and-effect explanation.

The brain compartmentalizes and correlates information to help us make decisions. In this way, feeling guilty is not bad if the guilt you feel is a true representation of the reality that your actions caused an unintended or, yes, even an intended effect. This kind of guilt motivates you to change future behaviors.

Sometimes our sense of guilt, however, can be false. For example, the brain of a child whose mother is drug addicted and fails to feed him may assign the reason for the neglect to himself. Perhaps it was his fault for not crying hard enough. In this case, his brain does not have the necessary information and draws a false conclusion. The truth is that Mom is addicted to drugs and is incapable of caring for her child's needs. No amount of crying can change that fact. What is reflected is not the true image of reality.

A student who does not get an A on a test may blame herself by concluding that she was lazy and did not study hard enough. However, the case may be that she suffers from an undiagnosed learning difference, such as attention deficit hyperactivity disorder (ADHD), dyslexia, or maybe even chronic fatigue syndrome. She actually did put in her best effort, but mitigating factors of which she was unaware were involved.

Let's face it: if you haven't already, you will make poor decisions as a parent. Your child will make poor decisions as a teenager. The process of assigning blame is only helpful if it leads to positive, constructive changes in future thoughts, emotions, and actions. In difficult situations, you should ask, "What do I need to change to make this situation better?" and "What does my teenager need to change to make this situation better?" When we feel guilty, we can use that guilt to help us reflect on these questions and move forward in a positive direction. Guilt stirs us to look for the partial cause and effect—our cause and our effect—in our present circumstances so that we can fix our part of the problem. Because our feelings of guilt may or may not reflect reality, we must not jump to false conclusions. We have to be intentional in our exploration and not make assumptions. In short, we must be teachable.

Learning from the Undead

Teachability is hard to incorporate into our parenting if we believe that admitting fault somehow undermines our authority. Sure, it can be embarrassing to admit when we are wrong, but our teenagers mature as much when they witness our teachability as when they observe our wisdom. Let them learn from your mistakes as much as from your successes.

When I was in medical school during my surgery rotation, we had lectures called M&M rounds. No, these were not as delicious as the name implies; quite the opposite, in fact. In morbidity and mortality rounds, an attending or resident physician presented a case in which a poor outcome had occurred. The purpose of the lecture was not to shame the doctors involved (though some of them were grilled pretty hard). The lecture was meant to be a learning experience for new and seasoned physicians alike, who were expected to grow in their knowledge and understanding of surgical procedures through studying mistakes. Guilt can serve a similar purpose as these M&M rounds do. Neither is pleasant to go through, but both are tremendous opportunities for learning and growth.

Even the apostle Paul recognized the value of healthy guilt. In writing to the Corinthian church, he said, "Even if I caused you sorrow by my letter, I do not regret it. Though I did regret it—I see that my letter hurt you, but only for a little while—yet now I am happy, not because you were made sorry, but because your sorrow led you to [change]."[1]

Unfortunately, healthy guilt can sometimes be confused with its evil stepsister, shame. Guilt says, "I did wrong." Shame says, "I am always wrong." Guilt says, "I made a mistake." Shame says, "I am a mistake." When we begin to associate ourselves with our failures, we have let shame take hold of us. The results are often devastating to our ability to parent well.

Running from Shame

Shame has a number of effects, usually on the extreme ends of behavior. First, shame leads to the extremes of impulsivity and/or passivity. When we tell ourselves we are inherently bad people, let alone parents, we let this thought process influence our decisions for the worse. For some, shame translates into paralysis. Believing that any decision made is going to be wrong, they refuse to act. They relinquish control to others—their kids, the media, teachers, peers, and other parents. They retreat into their own thoughts and obsess over future possibilities rather than deal with the situation at hand. They tell themselves, *I don't know what to do, so I will not do anything at all.* Or they believe, *I am bad, so I have no right to try to make my kids better.* For example, "Well, my kid now knows that I smoked marijuana as a teenager, so I can no longer enforce a no-drugs policy in my home."

When we feel that we have been disqualified by our failures, we are in danger of giving up on our kids.

Others take their shame and act impulsively on it. They think, *I'm a bad parent already, so what the heck?* Like the individual who cheats on his diet by eating a Big Mac and then decides, *Well, I've failed the diet, so I might as well order the fries and milkshake too*, parents who act impulsively out of shame tell themselves that because they lost their temper once, it doesn't matter if they do it again. Others too quickly jump to defend themselves when they face constructive criticism. Their impulsive defensiveness is a protective mechanism to avoid shame. Therefore they remain stuck in their failures and unwilling to consider valid recommendations that might actually help them turn the situation around.

On one occasion, I was speaking to a defiant teenager during a session with her mother. In my mind, I was defending the mother, trying to get the teenager to understand that no matter what mistakes her mother had made in raising her, she would not be able to use those mistakes as excuses for her actions toward others in the future. The teenager was claiming that her explosive rage was not her choice but rather the fault of her family dynamics. I was attempting to explain to her that her family dynamics may have contributed to some of her tendencies, but this did not excuse her bad behavior.

Later that day, I got a call from her mother, angry and upset at what I had said. "I literally felt like vomiting," she told me. I was shocked. "Why?" I asked. It turned out that after everything I had said, all the teenager heard was, "Your mom was a bad parent!" After I had a chance to clarify my statements—that I was not blaming her but simply acknowledging that all parents make mistakes, that I was actually trying to relieve her of some of the pressure of having to be perfect—she softened. She said, "I'm sorry. I've just been hearing from my daughter for so long how her problems are associated with my crappy parenting, I guess I'm pretty sensitive to it."

I applauded her for actually picking up the phone to discuss it with me. Many parents would have internalized my statements incorrectly and allowed them to deepen their shame, but it did prove a point: shame has the tendency to distort our interpretation of situations and often leads us to miss opportunities for positive change. The danger of shame is that it always allows our past to dictate our present and future decisions. We must be aware of this and take each situation as it is, not interpreting it based on our past.

Running from Blame

To protect ourselves from shame, one impulsive decision that parents make can be a fatal blow to a struggling zombie: we project our shame onto our children. Shame is such a powerful emotion that it is natural to want to get rid of it, to associate it with others. And our kids are an easy target. We become defensive and blame our kids for our misdeeds, in essence saying that we acted badly because they acted badly: "I lost my temper because you are so ornery." "I didn't enforce the rules because you are impossible to control." "I had to rescue you from this situation because you are too weak to take care of yourself." "How could you have been so stupid? I didn't raise you to be like this."

If we are not careful, we can find ourselves tearing down our kids with unconstructive, or perhaps even destructive and abusive, words. This further discourages them and leaves them with a sense of shame that pushes them into passivity and impulsivity, which leads to more self-destructive behaviors and deceptions. This does not have to be the case for you, but you must confront your own shame and challenge yourself to act contrary to the actions your shame is telling you to take. Here are some suggestions that might help:

Stay in the Present

The past is in the past. Don't allow yourself or your teenager to use the past as a means of controlling your present decisions. Take each situation as it arises and determine how to respond to it. Of course, I am not saying to ignore the past. If you know that you have made rules that you have struggled to enforce in the past, you can use that knowledge to create new, enforceable rules or examine new ways to enforce rules that are already in place. This applies to your teenager's actions as well. If you know that your teenager gets a speeding ticket every time he gets the keys to the car, you can use that knowledge to decide in the present if he needs to pay for a defensive driving course or if he needs a responsible adult to ride with him at all times. In this sense, the past can be helpful, but it is meant to inform present decisions, not control them.

When we allow the past to control us, we are acting on shame. We become like the woman who cut the ends of the roast off before cooking it because her mother and grandmother always did, not realizing that their tradition began out of a necessity that is now irrelevant: her grandmother did not own a big enough pot. In the same way, when we act out of shame from past failures, we invalidate our ability to change. Zombie teenagers feed on this insecurity. They love to use the

FACING OUR FEAR OF ZOMBIES

past against us. "But Mom, last week, you said I could go to the Wilsons' party. Now you are saying no. This is so unfair." "Dad, you let Jeff have a car at sixteen. Why can't I have one?" "Hey, you and Mom used to smoke when you were my age. I don't see the big deal." These are all tactics used to shift the focus off of the situation at hand and distract parents with feelings of shame in order to sway their decisions. As is true of all people, teenagers love to use your past decisions against you, but they would prefer that you ignore their past decisions when dealing with them. We all want judgment against those who have offended us and mercy from those we have offended. Your teenager is no different. Of course, whenever possible, it is good not to hold the past over your teenager's head. Don't let him hold the past over your head either.

When You Are Wrong, Admit It

A person with no scars is like a porcelain doll sitting high up on a shelf. You can admire him from a distance, but he is untouchable, unrelatable, and inanimate. When you allow your child to see your scars and he can freely show you his, that transparency establishes a life not free from some heartache, but one free from fear within the family. Don't be afraid of admitting your mistakes and making appropriate amends for them. To do this, you have to keep the true measure of success in mind: raising a teenager who is learning healthy and unhealthy choices and developing wisdom to fend for himself in this life. If your pride is more important than this goal, then you will never be able to admit that you are wrong. The inability to admit your mistakes presents a false picture of reality to your teenager.

First, it is confusing and frustrating to your teenager and

fosters anger and resentment. If everything you do is right, even when you are wrong, your child will be confused about how he should act as an adult. He will also learn that being right is always the goal, and that teachability is a weakness. I'm sure these are not qualities you want your child to possess. Sometimes the only way of teaching is by modeling appropriate responses after making mistakes. If you are teachable, your child will grow up to be teachable. The fear here is usually that if I am teachable, my child will use it against me. However, if you stay in the present and take care of your own shame, you never have to worry about this being a problem.

Don't Let Two Wrongs Make a Right

How we make up for our mistakes is just as important as admitting them in the first place. The consequences of our actions should fit the crime. Too often, parents feel badly about their own negative qualities they see associated with their teenager, so they excuse their teenager's behavior in order to feel better about themselves. "Oh, he is just passionate. I'm the same way. We just scream and yell when we have disagreements, but we always get over it. No big deal." Instead, if your son skips curfew and you happen to lose your temper with him, you should apologize to him but still follow through on your household rules. You shouldn't let your wrong negate the consequences of his. If you do, it teaches your child to manipulate. After all, if he can get you to lose your temper and that gets him out of punishment, what do you think he is going to try to do with you in an argument? That said, if you mistake your teenager's behavior and punish him unjustly, perhaps the best thing to do is to compensate him with a positive reward or activity to make up for it.

Get Used to Being the Bad Guy

Zombies resent the living and want to destroy them, even though they need the living to survive. Your kids need you, but they sure don't like you for it. For right now, you are the enemy. Be prepared to take a beating. It is easy to feel guilt and shame for failing to have your kids like you, but this is the reality that almost every parent experiences. Don't feel guilty about being the bad guy. Recognize that this is a season of life, and that someday, if you stay consistent and predictable in your actions toward your children, they will come to thank you for it in the end.

Case in point: I hated that my mother forced me to play the piano. I can't tell you the number of arguments we had about my practicing. Eventually, my mom relinquished control and stopped forcing me to play, but not before she had taught me the basics. To this day, I am grateful that she stuck with me. Playing the piano has become an incredible source of joy and relaxation in my life, and I would not go back and change the hours of frustration I spent sitting at the piano plunking away at the keys because my mom told me to. I guarantee you that the same will be true for your kids the older they get.

Have Grace and Mercy for Yourself in the Midst of the Process of Raising Your Zombie Teenager

When we rage in anger against someone, it is usually because we see a fault in the other person that we are unwilling or unable to accept within ourselves. We fail to accept the association. We shame others because we feel shame ourselves; we judge others because we feel worthy of judgment; we reject others because we are afraid of rejection. However, we love when we know we are loved. We can only love unconditionally when we know that we are loved unconditionally through the ups and downs of life. Grace for your children is born out of the grace you have first received from God, from others, and from yourself. Mercy for your children is given because you have received mercy. Structure and discipline are instilled within your kids because you have experienced their value in your own life. Be sure to recognize your needs, even as you attempt to care for the needs of your kids. If you do this, you will successfully navigate the guilt and shame within your own life and the lives of your children.

Now that you have some helpful tools for overcoming the guilt and shame of being associated with a teenage zombie, my hope is that you will stick it out and not give up. It's actually okay to be associated with a teenage zombie. It will make you more relatable as a human being and as a parent. And just think: if you stick with your teenage zombie through the tough times, you will be rewarded by his gratitude and love when he comes back to life.

Strategy Questions

1. In what ways is shame keeping you from acting as you should with your teenager?
2. What are some specific steps you can take this week to address that shame and prevent it from controlling your day-to-day decisions?

CHAPTER 8

The Fear of Exhaustion

In all zombie movies, the destruction associated with a zombie attack is of biblical proportions. The survivors always find themselves isolated, short on resources, and constantly under threat of further attacks. Physical exhaustion and raw emotions threaten to turn bands of brothers against each other. As a result of the destruction, the world is no longer a place of comfort and stability. It is harsh and cruel. The living must be stronger and smarter than their undead counterparts. They have to outlast the Spartan conditions of this new world. Many do not.

When dealing with undead adolescents, parents often feel like stranded survivors, barely getting by. Many just do not feel up for the challenge. It is easy to remember the days when your teenager was a baby. Problems were solved with simple solutions like the change of a diaper, a bottle of milk, a nap, or a special toy. You might have been physically exhausted, but at least her smiles and coos brought you emotional satisfaction. As she grew into a toddler, discipline was relatively straightforward. With a stern look or reprimand, a time-out or two, you could get your child to mind you. Of course, those days weren't without their challenges, but even parents with more defiant children had the advantages of size and a superior intellect.

Now, however, the situation seems dire. Your undead adolescent has turned on you and seems determined to tear you apart mentally, emotionally, even physically. The poor decisions she makes now cost you ten times more than any baseball thrown through a glass window or muddy footprint stomped on the carpet. Grocery bills pile up. Car insurance is expensive (especially after a wreck or two). College is expensive enough without having to repeat semesters for flunking grades or changing majors. If that were not enough, add in the possibility of having to deal with drug charges, pregnancy, bullying, or eating disorders. Watching your child suffer is emotionally exhausting. Attempts to offer solutions to her struggles are often met with resistance. Conflict becomes more volatile. Because she knows you so well, she can draw on your past failures as a parent to discredit your suggestions, undermine your authority, and ignore your discipline. On top of all of this, her words tear your heart out. "I hate you!" It's a statement no parent wants to hear, but most of us will at some point. No wonder parents are exhausted. The attacks of the undead always leave us wondering, *Do I have what it takes to survive this?*

The truth is that every parent feels this way at some point in the child-rearing process. Anyone who claims that she didn't is either lying or extremely lucky. She certainly can't brag about it, unless she is like people who brag about being tall! The truth is that if you are raising your child correctly, you are going to feel exhausted physically, mentally, and emotionally at times. The key is to notice the early warning signs of this fatigue and do something about it. Here are some helpful tips to get started.

Be Mindful of the Present

A lot of emotional energy is wasted on worrying about future events that never happen or past events that cannot be changed. Mindfulness is the process of staying in the moment, engaging your mind fully in the task at hand and setting aside all other issues or concerns for another time when they can be dealt with effectively. When I work with clients who are struggling with anxiety about situations in their lives, I ask them one simple question: "What can you do about this issue right now?" If the answer is "Nothing," I ask them to write down their concerns, set them aside, make plans to deal with them later, and then return to the task at hand. Anytime they find their minds wandering into the past or the future, they are to observe it happening, ask the same simple question and, if the answer has not changed, repeat the process of setting it aside and returning to the task at hand.

This can be very difficult at first, so it requires practice. I recommend not waiting until you are stressed about something to practice this form of mindfulness. It should be something you incorporate into your daily routine, just like taking a medication, eating a meal, or exercising. Yoga is an excellent and fun way to practice this skill. The exercises give you something to focus on while you de-stress and practice setting aside other issues for an hour. Prayer and meditation are also extremely valuable. Your ability to live one moment at a time in relative peace is strengthened when you force yourself to sit quietly and focus on a word of encouragement or the voice of God speaking to you.

The best way of describing mindfulness is by describing its opposites, which would be absentmindedness and the illusion of multitasking. Imagine if you had the television and radio on while reading a book and trying to listen to a conversation with your spouse—all at the same time. Your attention cannot be completely focused on any one of those stimuli; therefore, it is the same as if you were not focused at all. Another example is the daydream drive. If it is a route you have driven regularly, it is easy to get lost in your thoughts and forget the process of driving. By the time you get home, you almost don't remember how you got there.

Mindfulness is the process of tuning out all other distractions from your mind and focusing on the experience of the present. Try pretending that you are driving your route home for the first time. Pay attention to all the street signs, lights, houses, and traffic as if you could get lost if you didn't. This is mindfulness. It doesn't leave room for other thoughts.

Eating is an area where mindfulness can be useful. Try it. Practice eating a meal where you focus completely on the food, its taste, its texture, its smell, its appearance. Use all five of your senses and savor the process. Doing this allows you to slow down the process of eating, enjoy it fully, and avoid overeating.

Being mindful with our kids means staying in the moment when we are with them and letting them go when we are not. Let's say you are helping your daughter with her homework. I guarantee you that you start getting stressed when you think about how late it is getting, the conference you have to attend at work tomorrow, and the football game you are missing on the television in the other room. If you have chosen to help your child with her homework, what can you do about the other things you are missing? Nothing. So you can let those things go and focus on the task at hand. If you can acknowledge this, your stress levels will drop, you will avoid rushing your daughter through the process of homework, and you will be less likely to engage in conflict.

Sometimes mindfulness is just as important when your child is away from you. If you are cleaning the house while your daughter is at school and you find yourself worrying about who she is hanging out with or whether or not she is paying attention in class, you are not being mindful of the task at hand. Ask yourself, *If she is not paying attention right this moment, what can I do about it? Nothing.* So set the thought aside and deal with it later. Right now, the task at hand is to vacuum the living room.

The hardest time to practice mindfulness is when you are in the middle of conflict, an occurrence that may happen frequently if you have a zombie teenager. One of the goals of conflict resolution is to slow down the conversation to give people time to think. Any conflict management specialist will tell you that the time and setting for conflict resolution is extremely important. If you don't have enough time to resolve the issue, the conflict is likely to become heated, emotions will take over, and the objective will be lost. Frequent check-ins, time-outs, and clarifications are needed to make the process of conflict resolution effective. This requires mindfulness: mindfulness of your child's words, your words, her emotions, your emotions, how the words and emotions of each of you are affecting each other, and what the original purpose of the discussion was. Anyone in conflict can tell you how dizzying this can be without continual mindfulness. If you struggle with this, it is helpful to have a mediator or a counselor who can help infuse mindfulness into the discussion by observing, interjecting, and clarifying for you.

I have had to set a timer during intense discussions in order to give each person time to talk without interruption. Of course, focusing on what you are going to say next to prove your point rather than focusing on the words your partner or child is speaking is not mindfulness. As I've said, this takes lots of practice. Be honest and ask yourself if you need a coach to help you. Many therapists specialize in this area. Don't be ashamed to seek help if you are having trouble.

When you practice mindfulness, I guarantee it will help to reduce your overall stress levels on a daily basis. Of course, there are times to be mindful about the future. If we always stayed in the present moment, we would be like ostriches with our heads in the sand. Planning for the future is necessary, but set aside time to do it intentionally so that it doesn't infuse every other moment of your day. It may be necessary for you to set aside an hour in your day to worry. Yes, I said "to worry." It sounds funny, but I have actually recommended this to my clients who struggle with anxiety. "If you are going to worry," I tell them, "do it really well. Set aside an hour and worry your heart out, but when the task is done, move on to the next item on your agenda. If you find yourself worrying outside of that hour, tell yourself you are going to save that worry until the hour you have set aside for it."

You may not realize it, but the Bible actually addresses the subject of mindfulness. It says that whatever you set your mind to do, do it with all of your heart![1] This is the essence of mindfulness. Pour all of your attention and energy into the task at hand, and most issues in the future will take care of themselves.

Mindfulness also means being fully aware and thankful when life is good. Imagine a moment when your child is doing relatively well, when all things are in harmony and there are no pressing issues or fires to put out. Do not take those moments for granted. Cherish them. Bask in them. Do not worry about when the moment will end. Just soak it in for all that it has to offer, and you will discover that life has a lot more pleasant moments than you initially thought.

Understand the End Goal

What do you want for and from your children? Who or what do you need them to be? I cannot answer this question for you. Only you know. If you don't, there is work for you to do. Too many parents are unclear on the end goal for their kids, so they get caught up in the daily battles and forget the point of the war. So many parents I talk to say, "I just want my child to be happy." This isn't true, mind you, nor is it possible all the time. When you really dig deeply, you will discover that each of us has a lot of expectations for our children. Some are important and healthy; others are irrelevant, unattainable, and even problematic. The key is to be clear about them, clear to ourselves, and clear to our children. Parents who are not clear end up expending a tremendous amount of energy on unimportant issues because they are unsure of what they really want.

Some parents do have a clear vision of who and what they want their children to be someday. Exhaustion, discouragement, and hopelessness surface when these parents do not allow for any flexibility in their vision. Let me be frank: the more rigid your vision, the more disappointed you will be with your children. No one's—and I mean *no one's*—children turn out exactly the way he or she pictured. Certainly, we all have general hopes for our kids: that they will be kind, considerate, hardworking, successful, and of course, appreciative of all the hard work we have invested in their lives. But whatever your hopes for your children are, realize that there are negotiables and nonnegotiables in your relationship with them, and you must hold on to the negotiables lightly and be flexible. This will help you to expend energy more effectively in the long run. You will be less tired, having stored up your energy for issues that are really important to address.

Part of the success in resurrecting a teenage zombie is in letting her develop her own mind on the issues of life. This might mean that she chooses a different career, a different relationship, a different hobby or style of life than what you had in mind. She may have a different work ethic, a different disposition or personality, a different purpose for life, different struggles and joys, even a different way of living out her faith. None of these differences are bad for you or your child unless you have turned them into nonnegotiables for defining your success as a parent and her success as an adult child.

I know if you asked my parents twenty years ago if they could imagine their introverted and socially awkward son living a thousand miles away from home and working in private practice as a psychiatrist, they would have laughed. In fact, the first time I talked to my dad about my plans, he discouraged me from them (or, at least, he challenged me to consider the negatives). It took some convincing on my part to explain to him that this was the right path for me. This path has been fraught with challenges. I know that there have been times when both of us wondered if I had made the right decision. But right or wrong, it was the path I needed to travel, and he and my mom have supported me along the way.

Many parents expend a tremendous amount of energy trying to get their children from point A to point B in as straight a line as possible. The problem is that the path of life is never a straight line, nor is there always a point B at which we arrive. Parents who, in order to be satisfied, must have their children get straight As, go to an Ivy League university, major in biology, go to medical school, get married, and have two children, a dog, and a white picket fence somewhere on their property, will be drained mentally, emotionally, and physically in the end.

If you find yourself exhausted by your zombie teenager, it may be because your standards and expectations are too rigid. You are winning every battle but losing the war. With each conflict, your zombie teenager is growing stronger in anger, resentment, deviousness, and dependence. You may struggle with the opposite problem: you have no clear goals or expectations, so you have no idea what to enforce and what to let slide. As a result, you spend all your time putting out fires rather than fueling the right fires. You would be better off clearly defining your goals, modeling and explaining the principles you live by to achieve those goals in your own life, and creating boundaries and consequences for the nonnegotiables.

In the end, you cannot control the outcome, but you can reduce your fatigue and exhaustion in the process by being clear, consistent, and flexible where appropriate. A CEO told me that the employees who are the most anxious about their jobs are the ones who do not have a clear vision of what they are supposed to do. The same is true for parents and teenagers. Be clear on what is required and you will save you and your teenager a great deal of energy.

Celebrate Small Successes

Change is a gradual process and is almost imperceptible at times. If you are not paying attention to the subtle changes that are taking place in your teen, you wake up one morning and realize that, like a growing garden, everything in her life is in full bloom and you've missed it happening. If only we could see our lives unfold with time-lapsed photography, we might have a better appreciation for the changes taking place within our children. Unfortunately, we cannot, so it is easy to get discouraged by the imperceptible changes occurring in them. This is why celebrating small successes is helpful. It reenergizes us, helps us to realize that good things are happening, and challenges us to keep pressing on. A successful family is a family that never misses an opportunity to celebrate small successes. When we break life down into smaller chunks, challenges are more manageable, change is more noticeable, and failures are more easily fixed and set aside.

Imagine if you had to lose a total of 150 pounds in a year. Which is easier: Waking up every morning and thinking, *I have 150 pounds to lose this year.* Or waking up and telling yourself, *I have three pounds to lose this week.* Psychologically, the people who think in smaller chunks are the most successful.

The second reason why celebrating small successes is helpful is because it softens the pain of failures. So many adolescents tell me, "What I do is never good enough for my parents." I find that this isn't true. It is just that the parents don't say anything when things are going well. It is not that they are bad parents; they are just acting as firefighters. How many firefighters drive around town admiring all the houses that haven't burned down? For my tax dollars' sake, I hope none. If it isn't a volunteer group, they are most likely back at the station playing cards, sleeping, or taking care of other business. Many parents function the same way. When one child is doing well, they focus on the problems of the other kids or on their own struggles. Unfortunately, this sets up a precedent that says, "Success is not important. Failure is. We don't care if you succeed. We care if you fail." A child learns early on that if she wants attention from her parents, she must create waves. This stays with her into adolescence and beyond. Parents' help in times of crisis reinforces the child's dependency because it feels like love, so she begins to equate love with help. Parents feel this way as well. I love my children; therefore I must help them. Parents feel guilty leaving their children in pain because that has become the expectation of love from children who have grown to depend on it.

The key to celebrating is in providing variable rewards, anticipation of approval, and gradual escalation of expectations. Variable rewards are the most motivating forms of reward. Think of the person playing the slot machine. She does not know exactly when a reward is coming, but she anticipates it. That anticipation keeps her in the game. When the payoff does come, it is experienced as a combination of anticipation and surprise. I thought I could win, but I didn't expect it when it happened.

A gradual escalation of expectations means that you lengthen the time and extent of rewards as the child grows and matures. What was once celebrated is now expected because it has been ingrained into her normal behavior. Once that ingraining has occurred, external rewards are no longer needed. The child finds the activity rewarding in and of itself.

It is never too late to start celebrating your child's successes. You simply have to start where she is. If your daughter is currently failing her classes at school, you might celebrate with her when she pulls her grades up to a C. If your daughter is on drugs, you might celebrate with her a month of sobriety. If your child is afraid to fail, you might celebrate with her when she successfully navigates a failure in her life and owns up to it. Wherever your child is in life, look for ways to celebrate that life. It will energize both you and your child, and you will find that you have more strength to endure the tough times.

Let Consequences Work for You, Not the Other Way Around

Enforcing rules is probably one of the most difficult challenges parents face with their teenagers. It requires intentionality, persistence, and patience. Many parents find themselves setting rules and enforcing consequences, only to give up on those consequences after a few days or weeks of their zombies wearing them down with persistent attacks, arguments, and pushing of boundaries. It is exhausting work.

I remember when I was in high school, I got in trouble at a winter retreat our youth group took to a remote camp in southern Ohio. There was a lake outside the main pavilion where campers could ride paddleboats and canoes. We had been strictly warned that no swimming was allowed. The water temperature was too cold and there were no lifeguards on duty. Anyone on the lake had to be wearing a life vest. Of course, I thought those rules didn't apply to me. After all, I grew up swimming competitively and wasn't afraid of a little cold. What's more, a girl I had a crush on dared me to swim from the shore out to her paddleboat. What else could I do? (She was very cute!)

One of the youth leaders at the time was an older gentleman. He was ex-military, stoic, very firm, and not one to put up with any nonsense. When he found out about what I had done, he decided on an appropriate punishment: for the rest of the weekend, he had to be with me wherever I was in whatever activity I was participating. Big mistake! After several trips up and down the Sciotta Hills as I "changed my mind" between taking a nap in the cabins and playing soccer in the valley, he quickly realized that the punishment he had instituted was more work for him than it was for me. I give him credit: I think he lasted about two hours. Thankfully, when I see him today, we have a good laugh about it.

That story always reminds me that wherever possible, it is imperative that you create consequences that do the work for you, rather than you having to do more work. No parent is going to want to punish themselves for their kids' mistakes. If you are a parent who is caught in this cycle, you may need to be creative. You may want to sit down and discuss this with your spouse, a trusted friend, or a counselor experienced in arranging behavioral contracts. The key is to choose your battles wisely, but once you do, you have to fight to the death, and any ounce of reserves you can muster to make your life easier must be incorporated. I've heard some very creative ways of enforcing the rules from parents I have worked with.

One parent told me that because his son was unmotivated to study, Dad refused to pay for his college education. Instead, he made his son take out loans in his own name, and when the semester was over, he paid a percentage of the loans based on the grades his son had gotten.

After several warnings, another parent whose daughter had trouble being anywhere on time simply left her at home when she wasn't ready for a party they had planned, but not without disconnecting the Internet and locking down her cell phone first.

I have encouraged parents to do random drug screens if they are worried about their son or daughter using marijuana. Marijuana can be detected in urine for much longer than other recreational substances, and it is the drug most commonly abused by teens. Instead of punishing for positive tests, I encourage parents to reward for negative tests by reinstituting privileges that were taken away when the child's use was initially discovered. Why is this important? Because it puts all the pressure on the child to produce a negative test. If she wants the keys to the car, she must demonstrate that she is not using.

Now, of course, many parents ask, "What if my child is faking the test?" It is true, kids who are abusing drugs can be very creative about hiding their addictions, but many measures can be instituted with relative ease to assure that this is not happening. In the worst case scenarios, you can schedule your child for a visit to a drug testing lab, where blood or hair follicle tests can be performed. Having this scheduled may be a little more expensive, but it cuts down on your kid pestering you about when you are going to drug test her again. If the test does come back negative, you can go out to eat and celebrate, taking that time to encourage your child with positive affirmation and education on why you feel so strongly about the rules you have instituted.

If drug testing is a common and expected activity in your household, it cuts down on the "why don't you trust me" argument that most kids tend to use. You can simply say, "This isn't about you. It's just what we do!" This can also cut down on your worrying about your teenagers when they are out with friends. You know that you have a safe and effective means of checking up with them after the fact. If they know that this is part of the routine before they even leave the house, they will think twice about using when they are out with friends.

The key is to find out what your child wants and make her work for it. Start from a place of nothing and build on her efforts and motivation rather than starting her out with everything and pulling bits and pieces away as she fails. Incorporating this mind-set into your discipline will relieve you of a lot of blood, sweat, and tears.

The last point is this: though being the bad guy is necessary on occasion, the more you can take yourself out of the equation as the bad guy, the better. Establish treatment contracts ahead of time with your daughter, invite her participation in the process, and give her some say in how she should be punished or in what she can do to earn back privileges. This will give you ammunition in the time of conflict, because your daughter participated in the initial process.

It is easy to get discouraged. All of the above recommendations and examples might help, but they are not going to rid you of painful experiences with your child. You are still going to be tired at times. It is easy when you are exhausted to throw up your hands and say, "This isn't working," and give up. You will have successes and you will have failures, but do not give up on the process. It does work. Stick with it, keep trying, rest when you can, call in reinforcements when you need to, but don't give up. Failure always seems final, but it's not. If we buy into the hopelessness associated with a failure, we run the risk of failing over and over again.

Hopelessness is probably one of the most crippling emotions humans possess. Many parents draw on past failures to predict the outcome of current and future circumstances. Because they are tired, they act based on their predictions rather than on the possibilities, creating the very scenario they feared. They give in to their anger, shame, depression, or anxiety and let it rule the day. I see this in discouraged parents regularly. They look at the past, not to learn, but to do a postmortem analysis of sorts. They talk as if the game is over, the credits are rolling, or the last page of their child's life has been turned. Is it helpful to consider past mistakes? Certainly. But only to learn from them and change future behaviors, not to wallow in the illusion of an unchangeable future. Parents have to see the questioning of their performance as the halftime report rather than the post-game wrap-up. Do this, and every situation has the hope of redemption at the end of it.

Strategy Questions

1. What resources do you have at your disposal that you can use to help deal with the mental, emotional, and physical fatigue you're experiencing with your zombie teenager? How effective have you been at using them?

2. What attitudes and actions can you adopt to overcome the hopelessness you may be experiencing right now?

CHAPTER 9

The Fear of Humiliation

Have you ever noticed how cheap human life is in a horror film? Part of the guilty pleasure of a monster movie is watching an otherwise normal, everyday person being torn limb from limb by a swarm of savage beasts. No glory. No heroism. Just brutal, purposeless humiliation as the final memory of one's existence. We are terrified by it, but we can't look away.

Every human being has dignity, an inherent worthiness of honor and respect. From a Judeo-Christian perspective, dignity comes from being created in the image of God. Unfortunately, we lose our dignity when we act less and less like the design God intended for humanity and replace it with one that resembles an animal fulfilling the immediate passions of the moment without reflecting on our actions or considering the dignity of others. It is natural to want to hide our indignity. After all, Adam and Eve did it, and we've been doing it ever since. When our kids do undignified things, we feel the shame. We cannot help but feel that it is a humiliating mark on our parenthood and thus our character.

The isolation we feel when battling an undead adolescent is, in part, our choice. We would prefer to keep the challenges of resurrecting our children behind closed doors. If we could, we would lock them in the attic like Mr. Rochester's wife in *Jane Eyre* or follow the advice of Mark Twain and seal them in a barrel. We know too well what the prying eyes and wagging tongues of neighbors, church members, coworkers, family, and friends can do to our reputation and pride. No one wants to be the talk of the town, the subject of insincere prayer requests, or the freak show at the school carnival. When we open up to others about the problems we are having with our children, we run the risk of being judged negatively. When struggling with our teenagers' problems, we are vulnerable, not just to the abuses of our child, but to the degradation of society. If we reach out to "the village" for help, the "villagers" may come running to gawk at our fragility. If we open up, will people be respectful, appreciative of our honesty, gentle with our pain, empowering in our weakness, and as confidential as possible? We hope so, but the temptation to live in secret and avoid the embarrassment is always there. Here are some tips to help you confront this fear.

Face Your Pride

Being a parent is one of the most humbling experiences in all of life. I always find it interesting to hear celebrities talk about their kids. When asked if their kids understand what a big deal it is that their parent is a celebrity, over and over the reply is, "Nah, to them I'm just Dad. To them, I'm just Mom." It doesn't matter how popular, powerful, or successful you are, your kids have a way of putting you in your place.

There is nothing more humbling than acknowledging your shortcomings as a parent. After all, next to your spouse, your children are the people who know you best. They know that you have to put one pant leg on at a time in the morning. When they are struggling, it threatens your image in the community. The personae you have worked so hard to carefully maintain within society is at risk of being shattered. This is why many parents get scared by their children's actions and lash out in anger for control. They want to keep their kids from spoiling everything. Unfortunately, what they don't understand is that their kids are not idiots. They know this, and they can use it to their advantage.

One teenager I knew used to threaten to call the police and tell them that his parents were being abusive. The parents' fear that their child would do such a thing led them to give in to the child's demands. This scenario begs the question, "How important is your pride?" Secrets can always be used against us. If we have no secrets, no one can have any hold on us. The Alcoholics Anonymous community uses the expression, "You are only as sick as your secrets." This is true. The less you have to hide, the less you have to be afraid of.

Whenever I think about pride, I think of King David. He was the one who had an affair with Bathsheba and then had her husband, Uriah, murdered. I cannot imagine the embarrassment and shame that King David must have felt when the prophet Nathan called him out in public for his actions. But David confesses in Psalms that it was the best thing that ever could have happened to him. He says in Psalm 51 that before everything came out, he was so sick inside that it felt like his bones were wasting away. The relief that followed his confession was transformative. Certainly, David had a lot of challenges to deal with as a result of his decisions, but with transparency came freedom to deal with those problems in the open, rather than in secret.

It is also important to recognize that most of what we fear happening when we confess our struggles never actually happens. Take Bill Clinton as an example. When he was president, he was on trial for impeachment for his actions with Monica Lewinsky. Everyone was up in arms about it, but eventually, it became a nonissue. People are forgetful. Those interested in gossip and slander are always looking for the next juicy story. Is Bill Clinton's story a part of his legacy? Yes, it is and it always will be. But it hasn't affected his popularity through the years. In fact, he continues to be a spokesman for the Democratic Party and a frequently sought-after philanthropist and public speaker.

What is ironic is that when we are open about our humanity, we often become more likable to others. People are more interested in connecting with us because, right or wrong, they assume that our transparency means that we will be less judgmental of their struggles. The Bible verse is true, "Blessed are those who mourn, for they will be comforted."[1] Openness and transparency invite openness and transparency. So consider your pride. Is it helping or hurting you? Which would you rather have: your pride and no relationships, or relationships with people who know and understand that you are not perfect but love you despite (and sometimes because of) your humanity? It is up to you to decide.

Check Your Motivation for Sharing

If you have gotten to a place where you are willing to set aside your pride and seek help from the community, you must first understand your motivation for sharing. This will help you know who to share with, how much to share, and in what way. If you are seeking advice, then you must be open to constructive criticism. You will want to speak with someone who can relate to your struggle but has also demonstrated success in overcoming it. Understand that when you seek advice, you must be willing to consider the advice you are getting. Realize that you may not agree with everything you hear. Take everything with a grain of salt, consider that every situation is different, and know that ultimately the decision of what to do is up to you. If you find that you are getting defensive when you are receiving advice, then you may want to check your motivation again.

It may be that you really don't want advice but want someone to listen, understand, and affirm. If this is the case, you may want to consider seeking out a friend you trust who you know will not judge you, no matter what state you are in. Sometimes we just want someone to tell us he or she loves us no matter what. At other times we want to be challenged. We know we are struggling and we need accountability, someone who is going to check up on us and stay on us. In this case, you may want to consider joining a support group that has regularly scheduled meetings. Whatever your motivation is, you must realize that you are not always going to get what you want. Don't give up on the process. Keep searching, keep connecting, and keep checking your motivations.

Find the Right Community

Understanding your motivations for telling your story is important, but you also need to have an understanding of the kind of community that will be most receptive to the issues you're facing. Parents who have teenagers who are struggling with a mental illness or substance abuse will want to connect with a community that can provide effective support. Depending on where you live, these communities may be more or less accessible. Here in Dallas, I have a network of communities that I connect my clients with. Many churches have volunteer organizations like the Stephen's Ministry, Celebrate Recovery, or community groups that can help parents and teens connect. If you don't have access to a community, why not start one yourself?

Monica did exactly that. When her daughter died of an eating disorder, the loss was devastating, but she used that to fuel a passion for helping other families struggling with similar problems. As a result, she began a foundation in honor of her daughter. This foundation has sponsored fund-raising events, established a resource website, and provides numerous educational resources to her community.

In the zombie movies, people who stay still find themselves isolated and surrounded by zombies. If you keep moving and reaching out, you eventually find the people you need, and you can create a team to help each other.

Tell Your Story

Once you have acknowledged your hopes and expectations for opening up, begin to share. Realize that you are always in control of what you say. Many people give the thirty-thousand-foot flyover version of their struggle to determine how the recipient of the information will take it. The more you trust, the more you will be willing to share. It is important to recognize that telling your story benefits you. Talking it out allows you to analyze the situation in ways that you otherwise could not do. Having feedback helps you to gain insights, see things in a new perspective, and possibly approach the struggle in a new way. But telling your story helps other people too. It gives other people strength, especially those who are struggling with similar issues.

Rick was a well-known preacher in Kansas City who had been adamantly opposed to the use of medication for treating depression—that is, until he suffered from it himself. When he finally reached out for help from a psychiatrist, he was not too optimistic, but the medication worked. As a result of medication and talk therapy, his depression subsided and he began to speak about it in public. I remember hearing him speak about it at a conference I attended. He said that the more he opened up about his depression and use of medication, people from his congregation, his community, and at venues where he spoke would come up to him and confess that they were also struggling. People he would not have imagined were having an issue with depression confessed to him. Why? Because his transparency gave them courage to speak.

When you understand that people need to hear your story, it gives you a renewed sense of purpose beyond your own personal needs. This becomes an upward spiral as you recognize that your struggles give you a purpose, a legacy, and a connectedness with people you might not have thought possible before.

Start Early and Move Fast

The people who survive zombie movies are the ones who are constantly looking for help. They see the coming apocalypse, and they prepare for it by surrounding themselves with people who are resourceful and are going to be assets when times get tough. Know the people you need in your corner. Next we'll look at the types of people you will want to avoid and two people you definitely want to have with you when you or your child falls into problems.

Personalities to Avoid

Have you ever heard the song "Everybody Hurts" by REM? Well, it's true! We all go through difficult seasons in our lives. The people in our lives play a vital role in whether we have the strength to get back up on our feet and keep moving through life's journey. But consider the types of people who wait for us on the way down.

The Vulture

This person is openly antagonistic. He has been waiting for this moment as long as he has known you, and he has no qualms about letting you and others know his pleasure in your pain. This is the boss who can't wait to fire you, the frenemy who posts the embarrassing pictures of you on his Facebook account, the sibling who uses you to get in good with Mom and Dad, the church member who wants you out of the pulpit, the journalist who smears your public image. The list could go on and on. Nine times out of ten, the best option with the vulture is to keep your head high, ignore your antagonist, and distance yourself from any further interactions. Let your actions be louder than your words, be the better person, and trust that the vulture will learn his lesson from someone else someday. An old proverb says, "Don't cast your pearls before swine."[2]

The Vampire

Vampires are definitely antagonists, but in a subtler way. They pretend to be your friends, invite you to open up to them in the midst of your struggle, and then take advantage of you in your weakness. They are smooth and seductive but can't wait to suck your blood when they finally get ahold of you. They will use your weakness and vulnerability to drain you of your money, your connections, and any other resources they can sink their fangs into. Your suffering is only a means to accomplishing their own purposes in life. The way to protect yourself against a vampire is to hold your cards close to your chest. You might be suffering intensely and he always seems ready to help, but smile and make him believe you're doing just fine without him. Tell the vampire politely that you're not interested in getting together with him at his castle for dinner, because you know exactly who is going to be served up as the main course.

The Voyeur

The voyeur doesn't necessarily have a hidden agenda, but he will milk you for all the juicy details of your struggle. After a while, you get the sense that he really doesn't care about you. He just loves a good story. And trust me, someone who loves a good story is usually a magnificent storyteller too. The voyeur loves being in the know and spreading news. Hey feels better wallowing in other people's suffering. Here is one way to test whether or not someone in your life is a voyeur: tell him something exciting and positive that has happened in your life and see if he takes as much interest. You will know very quickly who your true friends are by who is able to celebrate with you, not just mourn with you.

Personalities to Manage

The Freak

The freak does not have a malicious motive. He simply "can't handle the truth!" (Imagine this being said in an aggressive Jack Nicholson voice.) Usually the freak is someone very close to you who suffers when you do. He loves you desperately, but *freaks out* when you're in pain. He is empathetic to a fault. You don't have to worry about him walking a mile in your shoes. In fact, you wish he would take your shoes off and give them back after one lap around the track, let alone a full mile. With these people, you may have to share burdens gradually over time. Let the issue sink in so that they have time to process it and come to terms with it. In doing so, you will create less damage in the long term.

The Fixer

The fixer is the opposite of the freak. Lots of solutions, very little empathy. I knew someone once who did informal counseling. She said, "Look, I'll meet with you for one session. You do what I say? Great! You don't? I've got better things to do with my time!" Now, to be sure, individuals like this might have a lot of helpful wisdom to pass on, but you need tough skin and the ability to take everything they say with a grain of salt. They have a cookie-cutter solution for every problem. Some advice might be worth chewing on, and some of it, well, in the words of comedian Jim Gaffigan, treat it like a Hot Pockets sandwich: "Take out of box. Place directly in toilet."[3]

Personalities to Embrace

We've reviewed the kind of personalities we want to avoid and those we need to manage when dealing with our failures. Let's take a look at two of the personalities we want to surround ourselves with during these times.

The Father

The sage. The guru. The sensei. An older individual who is not in competition with you has a deep yearning to mentor, and genuinely wants to be a listening ear and an adviser in your life. Draw from this person deeply, but realize that he may not be entirely able to relate to your circumstances. Every generation is faced with nuances in the suffering and pain they face. Culture, technology, styles, and relationships change over time, so look for a wise man or woman who is willing to remain teachable and empowers you to tell your story. Remember that as people age they naturally become fixers (minus the attitude), in part because they have had a lot of experiences we have not. The good ones remain humble in spite of all their knowledge. Hold on to them like precious jewels (or like your iPhone, these days)!

The Friend

A friend may not have all the answers, but he or she can relate to your struggle. A friend cares about you, wants to see you succeed, and will continue to walk with you every step of the way. There is loyalty here. A history. A brotherhood or sisterhood. You may have disagreements, but if someone butts into your inner circle, a friend will fall on his sword for you. Cherish these relationships. Be that kind of person to someone else. If you have one or two of these people in your life, you can weather any storm.

Reaching out and saying you need help is a humbling process. It is, however, essential to surviving a zombie attack as well as your child's adolescence. You are only alone if you want to be. Find your community and give as much as you get. Doing this, you will not only survive, but thrive through the good and bad times alike.

Strategy Questions

1. Who are the people in your life that you turn to for help and support in times of crisis? Make a list of the possibilities and ask yourself how you can foster deeper relationships with these people.
2. How have you been a help to others through the sharing of your triumphs and failures? How can you begin to practice being more open about your story as a means of helping others?

PART 3

Resurrecting the Undead Adolescent

CHAPTER 10

The Spark of Life: Motivation

Once you have successfully confronted your fears about having a zombie teenager living in your home, you can begin the actual process of resurrecting her. The first element necessary to resurrect your teenage zombie is to ignite the spark of motivation within her mind. This ignition begins when a teenager starts to understand herself—her passions and drives, her fears and anxieties, her strengths and weaknesses, and her hopes and dreams. This understanding comes through education and experience: an education on self-reflection and the experience of self-discovery. These are lifelong processes, but they have a particularly powerful effect on the trajectory of an individual's life during adolescence.

Before we can talk about the specific motivations of your child, we must talk about motivation in general. There are three truths of motivation we must explore. I believe that this general understanding will actually help you with the specific struggles with motivation your teenager may be having.

The first truth is that *motivation is evidence that we are alive and fully human.* When parents say that their kids are unmotivated, they misspeak. We are all motivated by something. To understand why we act, we must first accept that action is always preceded by a motivating and knowable force. This is why self-reflection is so important: if we know why we do what we do, we will have more control over our choices rather than allowing our choices to have control over us. Knowledge combats the mindless actions of a teenage zombie who might claim to be ignorant of a cause.

Once you accept the premise that actions have a knowable cause, the second truth is that *motivation has two key elements: pleasure and pain.* We will discuss these two key elements soon, but for now, simply understand that any action we take at any moment is influenced by one or both of these elements. Knowing this will defend against an assumption that we can act in a purposeless way.

Finally, the third truth is that *motivation has two primary environments—the world of accomplishment (work) and the world of accompaniment (relationships).* Understanding what drives your teenager in these two areas will help you channel her motivations through education and experience. Let's consider motivation as the evidence of the self first.

Motivation: Evidence of the Self

We know that zombies, the walking dead, have no motivation. They wander aimlessly through the world, purposelessly destroying everything in their path. The living, on the other hand, are inherently motivated. No action we take is purposeless. Everything we do has a reason. Our motivation is what defines us. Our hearts are, as the proverb says, "the wellspring of life."[1] Motivation is what points to the real you, your true self. The self is the sum total of your biology, psychology, spirituality, and experience. To understand the self is to understand what drives you and why.

Much of the challenge of adolescence is defining one's true self and then acting according to that definition. Adolescents are working to develop an identity that has integrity—wholeness and consistency—and that functions well in the real world. To do so, one must be able to reflect on one's thoughts, emotions, and behaviors and make determinations about this developing self: what parts to reinforce and what to change. For our zombie adolescents, this is the spark in their minds that begins the resurrection process. It is the transition from mindless, emotionally *controlled* behavior to conscious, emotionally *influenced* behavior.

When adolescents argue that they are not being selfish or that they did not think about what they were doing, they might actually be telling the truth. They feel the intensity of their emotions in any given situation, but cognitively, they do not understand nor can they articulate the reasons for their behaviors.

I cannot tell you how many times I hear "I don't know" when I ask teenage clients what thoughts were going through their mind when they made certain decisions. Because I understand that all actions have motivation and because I also know that most teenagers act emotionally without thinking, the goal of therapy is to help them discover the underlying motivation without judgment. With each exploration, the teenagers gain a little more understanding of themselves. There are several ways to do this.

One is to have clients journal their thoughts daily, keeping track of the various moods and emotions they feel at any given time. I ask them to make special note of the intensity of these emotions as well as the situations that triggered them. For those who really have a hard time feeling or expressing emotions, I give them a list of possible emotions to choose from. I might even ask a client to describe the location of an emotion in her body. One young woman described the annoyance she felt toward her little sister as a ringing in her ears. Another client described his anxiety as a catching in his throat that kept him from speaking, even when he knew what he wanted to say.

In addition to describing emotions, I ask clients to write down all the thoughts that run through their minds in moments of intense emotion. It is absolutely vital that clients do this each day, preferably shortly after incidents occur. When we reconnect for our weekly sessions, we review the thoughts and emotions that were triggered by the various situations and begin to explore the patterns we see. If clients struggle to put their thoughts into words, I might ask them to describe a mental image, a song, or a scene from a movie that would help to define their thoughts about a situation.

One young man described the helplessness he felt at the start of college with a scene from *The Hunger Games*. "It's like that moment at the beginning of the games when all the players have to race to the center of the lake to grab the weapons they will need to survive the competition. For me, not only would I not know what weapons to grab, but I don't even know how to swim, so I'm doomed from the start!" We used this scene to help him explore how overwhelmed he felt by the unknowns of college life, articulate what tools he really did have at his disposal, and then focus on the fact that, unlike the movie scene he described, his fellow students and professors were there to help him, not destroy him. The education of self-reflection led to an experience of self-discovery.

The truth is that you can do this with your son or daughter also. Too many parents try to confront their children in the midst of an intensely emotional situation and demand that the child tell them her thoughts. How can she when her emotions (and most likely yours as well) are controlling the situation? Instead, a weekly check-in with an adolescent in a pleasant atmosphere like a coffee shop or a park at a time when emotions have cooled, where parent and child can discuss the events, thoughts, and emotions of the week calmly can be an effective way of sparking the insight necessary for the adolescent self. The key here is consistency. Don't wait until a crisis arises to do this with your adolescent. Keep it as a regular appointment and your adolescent will feel less threatened by it.

"Selfless" Parenting Can Be Anything But

There are important reasons for parents to understand their own selves as well as their teens'. First, parents are not superhuman. In their relationships, they have wants just like their children. If we cannot acknowledge our self and its wants as we deal with our children, then we end up acting just as mindlessly as the zombies we are trying to resurrect.

Parents who find themselves in a power struggle with their teenager or young adult sometimes have trouble articulating what they want. To protect themselves, they couch their words in terms of selflessness. Some seem shocked or offended when I ask them, "What do you want from this relationship?" The most common response I get is this: "Well, I love my kids. I just want what is best for them. I just want them to be happy and success-ful." I try to explain to them that I cannot accept this answer as it is because it is incomplete. I challenge them to ask why they love their kids, why they want what is best for them, why they want them to be happy and successful.

Why are we so willing to sacrifice for our kids and not, let's say, for the neighbor's kids down the street? Because our kids are our kids! They are extensions of us, and therefore we experience their successes as *our* successes, their failures as *our* failures, their rewards as *our* rewards, and their pains as *our* pains. Because we feel so deeply for them, we might wrongly assume that every action we take is in their best interest, when in reality we might want something from and through them. This is where conflict arises. Despite the fact that our children are extensions of us biologically, psychologically, and spiritually, they might be very different from us. They have individual bodies and souls. What may be good and healthy for us may not be the best for our chil-dren. What we want for ourselves may not be what we should want for them.

One parent had to give up the hope of a son who would carry on the family business when the son decided to become a social worker instead. Another had to learn an unfamiliar cul-ture when her daughter decided to marry a foreign immigrant. Still another had to accept her son's move to another state to pursue the career of a lifetime. Choices like these require a relatively passive acceptance from parents, in some ways mak-ing them easier or harder to endure depending on the parent. Other challenges come when parents must make decisions that may go against the desire of their adolescent. For example, one parent refused to pay for an expensive private school and encouraged his son to go where he had a full ride instead. The parent acknowledged that he did not want to spend that kind of money, especially with two younger children who would need help also. The adolescent was left with the choice of getting a free ride or taking out loans to pay for his education.

I spoke with a man in his forties who recalled an interaction he had with his father that illustrates the effects of this deception of selflessness. "I love my parents to death, but I used to hate it when my dad would claim selflessness for his actions toward me. I remember when I was thirteen or fourteen, he bought me a really cool pair of football shoes. Shortly after, he stormed into my room, angry because of something disrespectful I had said to my mother. I am sure I deserved to be scolded, even punished, but he went further than that. He picked up the football shoes he had bought me, threw them at me, and shouted, 'How dare you treat us so disrespectfully. Especially when I just blew X amount of dollars on these shoes you wanted. We've bent over backwards to provide for you. Show some gratitude, will ya?'

"What Dad did not seem to understand was that *I hated football*. It wasn't my love. It wasn't my passion. It was his. He thought it would toughen me up. He valued strength as a quality within himself, so he valued it in his son as well. I played football from pee wee through high school, when an injury finally got me out of it. Were there benefits to football? Sure. I got good physical exercise. I developed some confidence that served me well in other areas of life. However, as a result of my interactions with my dad over football and other such disagreements, I also learned a passive aggression that has haunted me for years. I couldn't argue with my dad's 'selfless' actions toward me, so I learned ways of avoiding conflict with him and others like him instead."

None of us is perfect, but I believe we could save ourselves from a lot of pain and struggle with our kids if we would be humble enough to admit our own desires as they pertain to our children. Sure we want what is best for them, but let's admit that this is not as selfless a desire as we might make it sound. The most difficult conflicts of all are when you disagree morally with your adolescent's decisions and you know that her choice will lead her toward pain—for you and for her. Acknowledging what you want to avoid in this situation is just as important as the acknowledgment of what you want in others.

Though what we want may be in direct conflict with what our children want, it's possible that neither of us may be wrong. Too many parents with very strong convictions try to force their children into a specific mold, blinded by their desire to do what they think is best for their children, when in reality they are acting based on what they want. This, unfortunately, accomplishes the exact opposite of what they say they want to achieve: a child who is independently successful and capable of thinking on her own. Instead, you must be willing to step back, humble yourself, and rationally consider if your child's choices are really morally wrong or just go against your personal preferences. A good way to accomplish this is to seek out a trusted and unbiased third party, run the scenario by her, and see what she says about it. Be careful, though. You may not always get the advice or the opinion you want. You have to be ready to accept that and be teachable. I know many parents who seek out my services with the purpose of finding a yes-man, someone who will help leverage their biases and preferences against their kids. When I refuse to give them what they want, they move on to the next professional and start again. I always encourage parents to get a second opinion if they don't agree with my advice, but if you find yourself getting a third and a fourth and a fifth opinion, and you're still not satisfied with the answers you're getting, you may need to check your motivation.

Removing Guilt from the Equation

Second, renouncing the myth of purely selfless motivation absolves you and your teenager from false guilt and resentment. Think about it. If everything you are doing is always and only for your teenager, you place a tremendous weight of guilt on her shoulders when she decides to make different choices. Imagine the thought process of an adolescent forced to act out of guilt: *Wow, if Mom and Dad are killing themselves so that I can go to college to become an engineer, I guess I'd better go to college and become an engineer! I don't really want to, but I suppose I have to in order to make them happy. After all, if everything they are doing is for my happiness, I would be a pretty bad person not to follow through on it.* That guilt that your teenager feels will morph into resentment when she gets through college, becomes an engineer like you wanted her to, and recognizes that she hates her career. Ultimately, she will blame you for forcing her into it. Your words will come back to bite you when she says, "I thought you pushed me in this direction for me and me alone, for my happiness. So why do I have to do it if I am not happy?"

Think also about the guilt and resentment you might feel toward your child if you continue to sacrifice yourself on the altar of your child's happiness but she isn't happy. When you step back and consider that you don't have to kill yourself in order for your child to turn out well, you lose the guilt and empower her to make her own decisions. This way you can avoid burnout, and maybe even have more strength over the long haul to help her handle problems as they arise.

The Elements of Motivation: Combating Meaninglessness

Motivation is both easy to define and very difficult to understand. As a whole, your motivation is your answer to the question, "Why live?" It is the spark that brings life to all of us. When you see bumper stickers that say, "I Live for the Weekends" or "I'd Rather Be Golfing," the driver is revealing to you, at least in part, his life's motivation. The question that all of us, including our adolescents, have to answer is, "What do I live for? What is the driving force of my life?" If only the answer was simple enough to fit on a bumper sticker, parents and children could be saved from a lot of conflict. But our motivation for life is multifaceted, constantly shifting, and influenced at any given moment by our biology, psychology, and spirituality. The more we understand these influences, the more conscious control we can have over our behaviors.

Parents in my office complain about how unmotivated their teenagers are:

> "I just can't get him to do anything. I've asked him to pick up his room, take out the trash, do his homework, be kind to his siblings, or get a job. Instead, he sits there on the couch, watching TV and playing video games. He just doesn't care!"

"I can't understand why my daughter wants to cut herself, starve herself, spend hours in her room listening to sad music, and stay up late into the night texting her friends and surfing the web."

"My son or daughter is just so unmotivated."

I am quick to point out to these parents the falsity of their conclusions and ask them to clarify what they mean. Their children may not be motivated to do the specific activities the parent has listed, but they do not lack motivation in general. Your challenge as a parent is to discover what elements of motivation are leading your child to behave the way she does. If you accept this challenge, then unlike the Hollywood horror flicks, you will have the power necessary to resurrect your teenage zombie back into a living, breathing, thriving human being with purpose and devotion.

There are really only two elements to motivation. I will tell you what those are in just a moment, but let's first consider what they are not. To illustrate, let me walk you through the steps I use when teaching counseling students.

First, I ask them to stop analyzing their clients for a moment and focus their attention on themselves. I ask them to tell me what makes them motivated beings. The room is usually silent for a few minutes as the students think. When they've had a chance to process their thoughts, I usually get answers like the following: my religion, my job, my children, my boyfriend or girlfriend, my spouse, my ministry, my hobbies, my education.

Once we have generated this list, I explain to them that none of these elements are *essential*. Sometimes we are motivated to serve our children, and sometimes we are not. Sometimes we are motivated to do our absolute best at our jobs, and sometimes we are not. We lose interest in our hobbies, and we fall in and out of love with significant others. I will usually tease students about their grades and say that sometimes we are motivated to pursue a good education and, well, sometimes we are not. Even God, the Creator of all things, is not the motivating force in our lives at all times.

As parents, this truth should bring you an incredible amount of relief. Step back and consider this: you are not responsible to be the motivating force in your children's lives, and you do not have to resent your children if they are not always motivated by their love and affection for you. How might this change the way you have engaged your zombie teenager in the past, and how might this affect the way you plan to deal with them in the future? As parents, we can create environments that foster or discourage our children's motivation, but we cannot be the source of their motivation. Too many parents feel guilt over their inability to change their kids. As good parents, they think they should be able to. We can't!

So if all of these good things in our lives are not essential elements needed to have motivation, what is essential? Some students come close when they say purpose. Purpose is an essential element of motivation, but it depends on how you define it. It can mean that which you *want* to achieve through your actions (desired purpose) or it can mean that which you *should* achieve through your actions (expected purpose). When your desired purpose lines up with your expected purpose, everyone is happy. But when what you *should* do doesn't line up with what you *want* to do, conflict ensues. Motivation, then, is always the purpose you *want* to pursue at any given moment in time—also known as your affections, your desires, your passions. It is feasibly impossible to do something you do not want to do.

I know this sounds confusing. People say things like this all the time: "Well, I didn't want to go to the gym today, but I knew if I didn't, my doctor would be upset, so I went." This does not mean you did something contrary to what you wanted to do. It means you had two wants and the one you wanted more won out. You wanted to please your doctor more than you wanted to avoid exercise. No one has ever done anything in life simply because she *should* have done it. This is why therapists always tell their clients, "Stop should-ing on yourself." (Yes, the pun is intended.)

For example, as a parent, maybe you thought far enough in advance to consider that by having children you could have someone to care for you in your old age. That would then be your children's expected purpose placed on them by you, their parent. You could then say to your children, "The reason you are alive today is so that you can fulfill your purpose of being my caretakers in retirement." Now, if you have treated them well, taken care of their needs, and fostered a loving, healthy relationship with them as they grow, then they might adopt this expected purpose and make it their desired purpose for themselves. But if they don't, you'd better check out the nursing home down the street. (Just sayin'!)

Of course, this is a humorous example, but the problems you are having with your teenager are because your expected purpose for her does not align with her desired purpose for herself. If you were okay with her lounging around the house all day, failing in school, doing drugs, and mooching off your hard-earned resources, there would really be no point in your reading this book. We would all love for our kids to do what they are told to do just because it is right, but if that is your expectation, you will be or have already been very disappointed.

It is true, then, that our desired purpose (our motivation) at any given moment drives our thoughts, emotions, and actions. If your motivation in the moment is your children, your significant other, your job, or your education, then that will be the motivating force behind your actions. But desired purpose has two components that define it: (1) the acquisition of a reward and (2) the avoidance of pain. When our expected purpose as a child, husband or wife, employee, student, or person of faith does not align with our desired purpose in the moment, it is because our understanding of the reward for fulfilling our expected purpose does not seem worth the pain.

This is exactly the problem for your kids. I guarantee you that if you were to ask your kids, "Do you want to be a good student, a good child, a successful worker, a well-liked friend, etc.," they would all say yes. Then why aren't they? Because a more immediate or satisfying reward or comfort is interfering with their stated desires.

Let us explore this concept more closely. Remember, any action we perform in life has a reason. "I don't know" is not an answer. Have you ever asked someone why she did or did not do something and she responded with, "Oh, no reason . . ."?

"Why did you buy that new car? The one you had seemed to be working great."

"Oh, no reason. I just felt like it."

"Why did you spend all day playing video games? I thought you were going to do your homework."

"No reason, really. I just felt like it!"

"Why didn't you look for a job today? I thought you needed one."

"Oh, no reason. Something else came up."

To avoid "I don't know" answers, sometimes I have to rephrase the question and make it less open-ended. Instead of asking, "Why did you do X, Y, or Z?" I might ask questions like these:

- What did you hope to gain from the purchase of a new car?
- What does having a new car mean for you?
- What do you get from playing video games that you do not get from doing homework?
- What would you stand to lose if you did your homework before playing video games?
- What does staying home today help you to avoid?
- What is looking for a new job going to cost you?

Notice how these questions get to the heart of the potential reward or pain that the individual wrestles with in any given decision:

- If I stay in the safety of my home, I can avoid the potential rejection I might face from a prospective employer.
- If I spend all day playing video games, I can feel like I am accomplishing something with a lot less effort than doing my homework would require.
- If I buy a new car, I can get an immediate sense of

identity, power, and control that I have not felt otherwise in my daily life.

The key is to discover what reward your teenager is acquiring or what pain she is avoiding in her actions.

Now, a teenager's reward might be nefarious. If she is angry or resentful toward you as a parent, her reward might be to see you get angry, flustered, or confused. She might enjoy seeing you helpless and out of control, so she argues and defies any rules you try to impose on her. We hate to think about our kids being so cruel, but after all, they are zombie teenagers. They can't help it, right?

It is also true that the pain in teenagers' lives that they are trying to avoid could be healthy pain. School is taxing. Jobs are stressful. Relationships take work. They challenge us physically and mentally, but in the process of experiencing pain, our muscles grow, our wisdom increases, and our good standing with people flourishes. Zombie teenagers can't fully grasp this. They are either too burdened by the pain in their lives or too comfortable to risk a discomforting situation to achieve more. This is where we as parents can step in and help our teenagers understand the pleasures and pains that are at stake and challenge them to consider whether enduring the pain or pursuing the pleasure will be worth it for them in the end.

The Environments Where We Are Motivated

In zombie movies, cities that have been overrun by a zombie attack are cordoned off into districts that represent places of safety and places of danger. The purpose is to contain the threat, help survivors find safety, and rally for a defensive action or counterattack. To remain alive, it is crucial that you know these districts.

For our purposes, these districts represent the areas of a teenager's life where motivation is crucial. Fortunately, there are only two of them. In describing them, I am using the presupposition that they are inherent needs we all have as humans. It's beyond the scope of this book to explain why we have these needs. Instead, I'll just say that we need them because we need them. My philosophy stems from a Judeo-Christian worldview, which says that men and women were created in God's image. Because God is a creator, we seek to create. Because God is relational, we seek to connect with others. Because of this, our motivation is focused on these two areas of our lives. The ways in which this motivation is expressed is multifaceted, but the basics of the motivation are inherent to all human beings.

District 1: The Business District, or Our Accomplishments

The Business District is where your teenager experiences a sense of accomplishment. It is the task-oriented side of your adolescent's identity. We, as humans, were created to work.[2] Inherent in any activity, even fun activities, is the sense of fulfillment and accomplishment we feel when we work at a task and complete it successfully. For example, when your son sits down to play a video game, he experiences satisfaction after completing a level or earning a certain number of points. This experience may be immediately more gratifying than sitting down to draw symbols on a piece of paper (algebra) that over several weeks will eventually earn him another symbol (A+) that has absolutely no meaning to him other than the fact that if he gets enough of these symbols, he can go to a place far away (college) where he can spend hours working to get more of these symbols that will eventually earn him more work (a job). He's asking, "What's the point?"

Ironically, playing the video games actually provides a more meaningless reward, just packaged differently. In many games, players can go to auction sites and purchase "bling" for their characters. These are items that do not do anything to help you accomplish the tasks of the game, but are simply status symbols to make other players jealous. These items can be bought and sold with real money through PayPal accounts or with Bitcoin. These rewards are utterly meaningless except for the meaning that the players ascribe to them. They provide what we call "token economy" to those who are immersed in the culture of the gaming world. So even here, humans cannot escape materialism, status, power, success, and the pursuit of rewards.

There are other examples of the pursuit of more immediate rewards at the sacrifice of better future rewards:

- A girl who restricts herself from food can see the more immediate results of a slender body without understanding the long-term harmful effects of malnutrition.
- An athlete who takes steroids may perform better on the football field in the short term, but fails to understand how he will be limiting himself in so many other ways as

a middle-aged man facing infertility and the need for a kidney transplant.

- A student who cheats on an exam in order to get an A will find that when she gets the job of her dreams, she will be unable to recall the information needed to perform well.

The point is that no matter what people do, whether it's for business or pleasure, satisfaction comes through the sense of accomplishment we get from working toward an achievable but challenging goal. Your child will naturally pursue activities that provide that right amount of challenge for the skill set she currently possesses. If the challenge of a task is too great for her skill level, she will have anxiety and get discouraged. If the challenge is too low, she will get bored and distracted. When the challenge matches her skill level, she will experience what positive psychologists call *flow*, a total immersion in the task at hand.[3]

If your child appears unmotivated to pursue a particular task, it could be for a number of reasons. One is that she finds the task boring. The process is not stimulating enough for her to stay on track, and the final reward for completing it feels insignificant or pointless. The other reason she may be unmotivated is because she deems the task too hard and experiences discouragement and anxiety, which causes her to drift to other more rewarding or less challenging activities. Finally, she may not understand the level of pain or the missed opportunities that are headed her way if she does not complete the task. Parents can help generate flow in their teenager's life by creating environments that balance the levels of pleasure and pain they experience in any given activity. A parent can provide rewards and consequences. A parent can provide education on the ultimate purpose of activities. A parent can allow room for experiencing pleasure and pain in the teenager's life. We will discuss how to do this in the section on pulse, but hopefully, at this point, you are beginning to see why this knowledge is crucial for you and your teenager. Knowing the nature of motivation is essential for sparking it within your teenager's pursuit of accomplishments.

District 2: The Public Square, or Our Accompaniment

The second district encompasses our relationships. We all have an inherent need to love and be loved by others, and to belong to a group. For some of us, this need is greater than others, but the need itself is inherent to being human. Even the most introverted people feel the need to connect once in a while. There are great rewards to be achieved from relationships. To be known, accepted, and empowered, we must have people in our lives. We find physical and emotional support from others. Complementary qualities and needs provide the opportunity for sharing. The feeling of being remembered is a gift only the presence of another can provide. If God said it was not good for mankind to be alone, then we must believe there is something inherently valuable about the presence of another person in our lives.

Relationships, however, bring pain too. They open up the door for rejection, betrayal, selfishness, misunderstandings, and conflict. When your teenager ventures out into the public square, she hopes to be rewarded with acceptance, significance, understanding, and support. She wants her qualities to be welcomed and desired, her contributions to be important, her struggles to be felt and understood, and her power for success to be greater than what it was when she was alone. The pain in this district arises when, instead of feeling accepted, she feels unworthy; instead of feeling significant, she feels unimportant; instead of feeling understood, she feels misunderstood; and instead of feeling supported, she feels torn down. If your teenager has a high frustration tolerance born out of a stable identity and a clear vision of the long-term rewards of healthy relationships, she may be able to endure these hurts and enter into truly satisfying relationships. However, if your teenager has a low frustration tolerance, she may seek to secure more immediate versions of these rewards through the objectification of people, or seek to avoid more pressing, seemingly intolerable pains by isolating herself. Parents must model, educate, and empower their teenagers to engage others and recognize the potential pain, but also the inherent reward, in loving and being loved.

We will continue to explore these concepts in the last two chapters. For now, however, recognize that to be motivated, teenagers must have a spark of self-awareness, understand the pleasure and pain that guide their day-to-day choices, and begin to understand that some rewards are worth the pain and others are not. Through education and experience, they will come alive to the good things that life has to offer them when they approach it with mindfulness and meaning.

Strategy Questions

1. Make a list of the expected purposes you have for your teenager and the desired purposes she has for herself. Where do they align and where are they different? What are the negotiables and what are the nonnegotiables? What can you do to compromise on the negotiables and motivate your child toward the nonnegotiables?

2. Consider what currently motivates your child in the business district and the public square. How can you begin to use those things to help motivate your child toward other healthier pursuits?

CHAPTER 11

The Pulse of Life: Direction

As we begin to discover the spark of life that exists in each of our teenagers and the motivations of pleasure and pain that move them moment by moment, our job as parents is to help them contain these drives and channel them in a healthy direction. In other words, we must revive a pulse within them to give them life. Pulse is what contains our passions, establishes direction for our lives, and creates order instead of anarchy and chaos. It helps generate resiliency in tough times, and it provides a common language and worldview so we can understand where we agree and disagree with others. With a strong pulse, we move toward a greater good beyond what feels right in the moment. Unfortunately, establishing pulse within our teenagers requires conflict, and conflict is extremely exhausting. The stronger *your* pulse is the more energy you will have to face the conflict and establish a healthy pulse within your teenager.

In medical terms, our *pulse* is the pressure we feel exerted against our blood vessels when blood is pumped by the heart. To generate a pulse, there are actually two conflicting forces at work: the systolic pressure (the pressure exerted by the blood against the blood vessel walls when the heart contracts) and the diastolic pressure (the pressure exerted by the blood vessel wall on the blood as it reverts back to the original diameter it had when the heart was at rest). Without one of either of these pressures, you will not have a pulse.

There is an equivalent pulse necessary for our teenager's psychological, social, and spiritual survival; it is the conflict that arises when a teenager's passions push against the opposing rules that contain him or her. This moral or ethical framework keeps a teenager's passions contained, tempered, and headed in a healthy direction.

Pulse is important because the best rewards in life are not always the most immediate ones. Likewise, there are some constraints against passion that are worth enduring if they prepare us for something better in the future. Just as our bodies need a strong pulse in order to nourish the parts that are farthest from our hearts, so too we need a strong pulse for life in order to keep us from settling for more immediate pleasures when a more lasting happiness awaits us in the future.

As you know, teenagers are always testing boundaries, trying to determine what is permissible and what is not, and what they can get away with without getting into trouble. The phrase "That's not fair," I am sure, has been repeated in your home more than a few times. It doesn't matter what rules you have established; most teenagers will question them, demanding more and more freedom as they grow older and eventually head out on their own. They will need an appropriate level of pushback from you in order to generate the forward momentum they need to reach lasting goals and rewards. With pulse, we have a guide to help us navigate. We have an established system for understanding right and wrong, good and bad, healthy and unhealthy, better and best.

Pulse Solidifies an Enduring Self

While our spark—our motivation—is evidence of a transient self at any moment of time, our pulse—our direction—creates a molded and solidified self that endures over an extended period of time. It is what we might call "character." Like spark, pulse has two environments or districts in which it is needed: the business district and the public square. For example, there are limits set on our accomplishments in business—limits on how we can achieve our goals and limits on what goals we can ultimately achieve. If a goal of ours is to be financially secure, we must abide by the limits imposed on us by the Internal Revenue Service, the Better Business Bureau, and the person who pays our income. There are also limits on our personal relationships: what we can receive from and give to others. If we want romance, we cannot force it on someone who doesn't feel that same passion for us. If we want self-confidence, we cannot constantly be borrowing from the confidence of others. When we come to terms with these limits and act consistently within them, our identity solidifies. We develop integrity.

The Challenge of Making Decisions

One of the benefits of having a healthy pulse is that it allows us to make decisions quickly and confidently. Think of how much mental and emotional energy we would expend in order to make relatively simply decisions throughout the day if we didn't have an established rubric to follow. Let's take a relatively straightforward choice: what to have for breakfast. This decision, first and foremost, is sparked by the desire to pursue a reward (food) and avoid pain (hunger). If you are in a rush and you want something immediately satisfying with as little hassle as possible, you will choose something quick, easy, and delicious. In this case, donuts are a great option. However, if you put any thought into the potential consequences of this choice, your pulse is already kicking in: *If I eat a donut, will it sustain me until lunch? Will I feel sick from all the sugar? How will it affect my weight and energy levels?* You are now moving beyond the immediate rewards or pains and focusing on the potential future rewards or pains your decision may incur.

Perhaps you decide that it might be better to choose something healthier, something not as sweet. *Well*, you think, *I could make myself an omelet.* But at what cost? An omelet takes more time. You would have to wake up earlier to avoid being late for work. You would have to plan ahead and buy the necessary ingredients to make it. You would have to sacrifice your craving for sweets in that moment.

There are other questions that must be answered too: *Is one donut really going to make a difference in my overall health? In my well-being? In my long-term success? Do I really want to change my routine for the morning and try something new? After all, I've gotten comfortable with donuts, even if they aren't the healthiest. To change would require work. What's more, why do I really need the extra energy? How important is my job, my health, or my cravings? Why should I be concerned about being healthy anyway? Life is too short. I should enjoy every moment of it, right?*

Notice how we've only talked about one choice in a day, and a fairly simple one at that. If we had to go through this rationalization consciously every time we made a decision, no one would do anything. Our pulse is always working in the background. When we postpone pleasure for a greater reward or we willingly face pain and suffering in the moment to accomplish something worthy, we are acting based on the pulse of our lives. The same is true when we refuse to indulge in a momentary pleasure because of the future pain we know will come, or we decide that current sacrifices in our lives are not worth the future rewards awaiting us. When we lose sight of the end goal, when the pressure of our current circumstances rises above what we can handle, or when immediate consequences do not seem important, we risk losing our pulse and bleeding out. People with a strong pulse, however, will want to do now the things that they have to do in order to have later the things that they want to have.

When and How Does Pulse Begin?

Our pulse begins to develop from the moment we are born. All of us are born with an innate set of drives or passions. Immediately upon entering the world, these drives within us begin to assert pressure on our environment, and our environment asserts pressure on us. We learn how to deal with this pressure in two ways: (1) through experience by trial and error, and (2) through our interpretation of each of our successes or failures in dealing with the pressure. Over time, our experiences and the meaning we ascribe to them shape our worldview. This worldview becomes the framework by which we channel all our passions. Let's explore this further.

At the beginning of our development, pleasure and pain signals have no encoded meaning in our brain's hardwiring beyond the immediate sensations we feel. As babies, all we know is what feels good and what feels bad. Freud described these collections of drives as our *id*.

Over time, however, our experiences influence the way we judge our bodily sensations and the way we seek to acquire pleasure and avoid pain. This external regulation from the environment generates an overarching framework or worldview that Freud described as our *superego*. The very first and most significant relational influence on our superego is, of course, our relationship with our parents. This superego is something that is gradually internalized within our minds over time as our brains experience, process, and store each successive parental reaction to our behaviors.

The ego comprises the functional elements of our minds that we use to manage the budding conflict between our id (our basic human desires) and our superego (our acquired inhibitions). They include a mixture of natural predispositions such as our baseline intelligence quotient (IQ) and memory capacity, as well as nurtured potentials like our ability to tolerate frustrating experiences, our ability to express ourselves through language (the ability to talk out versus act out our emotions), and our defensive behaviors (the ways we learn to deal with threats to our understanding of ourselves). Over time, parents and children act upon each other, mutually influencing the other's thoughts, emotions, and behaviors.

An early example of this process might occur during a routine diaper change. Imagine a child reaches down to touch his genitals, a natural act of self-exploration. His mother, disturbed by the action, smacks her child's hand and says, "No, no." If this mother's response to her son's behavior is repeated regularly, the child learns through conditioning that, whatever the initial reason for his behavior, touching himself will be followed by a painful experience, at least when his mother is present. He learns that there is a cost involved. This fundamentally changes the child's experience.

But the child also attaches a meaning to the experience. Early on, the meaning may be simply "This is bad" or "This hurts." As he grows older, further meaning is ascribed as similar situations arise. He learns attributes like modesty, shame, respect for privacy, and social acceptance. Each new interpretation of an experience is stored in his brain for reference to help him determine how to act in the future. In point of fact, the environment (his relationship with his mother) changed his mind (his brain's basic understanding of pleasure and pain).

We must consider the opposite influence as well: the child's influence on the environment. The child's most likely response to his mother's punishment is to cry. If his crying is intense and prolonged, it may have the effect of generating guilt within his mother. The mother's guilt leads her to change her behavior. Instead of inflicting further punishment, she might reward her child with a special treat in order to assuage her guilt and his pain. This now creates a new experience for the child to process. He sees that crying as a response to pain elicits sympathy and reward from the initial perpetrator of that pain. He may then use this reaction as a means of avoiding further punishment in the future. In this way, the cycle of mutual influence continues. Each successive experience of pleasure or pain builds on the one before it, such that the environment, acting on the brain, in essence creates a new brain (no matter how subtle the difference) that then engages and shapes its environment in a new way.

Fast-forward fifteen years and imagine two different relationships. One is a relationship between a mother and son that has perpetuated a cycle of shame and guilt. The boy, who is now a teenager, has learned to hide his behaviors from his mother very well. So well, in fact, that she, not knowing that her son was even sexually active, is shocked to discover that he had been dating a girl he met online for the last year and had gotten her pregnant. She found out only after being notified by the girl's parents, who called to tell her son to stay away from their family. This may sound like an extreme example, but incidents like this happen more than you think. Many parents would be shocked to find out things teenagers tell their therapists that they would never disclose to their parents, not because they don't want to be open with their parents but because the pulse of shame has solidified over time.

The second relationship looks something like this: both mother and son have responded to each other over time with consistent but flexible reactions. At fifteen, the son knows that his mother feels strong emotions toward his behaviors, good and bad. He also knows that she is willing to process and temper those emotions with him, treat him with respect and dignity, and be intentional about the decisions she makes that concern his life. Likewise, he talks to her openly about anything, trusts her wisdom and honesty, and adopts a level of self-discipline born out of the principles she has taught him over the years. He has a girlfriend, but they've decided to wait on sexual activity because they have longer-term goals they don't want to risk losing.

There are many other examples of how our pulse solidifies over time. For example, the meaning that parents, friends, and the rest of society ascribe to the talents we possess as children will affect the way that we judge our interests, abilities, and pursuits as adolescents and adults. A boy who enjoys arts, crafts, and fashion may feel guilt and shame if he is taught that these are not masculine pursuits, but if his parents admire his creativity and provide opportunities for him to pursue it, he will take more pride in his work. An athletic girl might never develop a passion for sports if a mother's obsessive fears of injury are ingrained into her psyche, but if Mom processes her anxieties elsewhere and presents a posture of courage and faith in the presence of her daughter, the girl might learn to accomplish more than she thought possible on her own. An outgoing child might learn to suppress urges to be gregarious if strict parents believe that children should be seen and not heard, but if they make room for his talkativeness, he might just develop the confidence necessary to succeed in the marketing world. An adventurous child might become timid after experiencing a traumatic accident that is deemed her fault, but she also might become a good counselor if she is given the tools to accept and move past the trauma.

Eventually, over time, our brains and environment cooperate to create a solidified and predictable interpretation of life's experiences. Follow this process of mutual influence—the environment on the brain and the brain on the environment—for ten, twenty, or thirty years, adding on new relationships, places, and events, and you can easily see how the compounding experiences of a person's life hardwires a pulse around the spark of his or her natural drives. This becomes the complex essence of an individual: the unspoken rules by which we live.

Matching Pulses

Despite the influence that parents have on the development of their children's motivation, many people are too quick to blame a zombie teenager's failing pulse on poor parenting. This is a much too simplistic understanding of human experience. To begin with, children are born with differing dispositions. A child who is naturally compliant and easygoing can make parenting a relatively painless experience, bringing pleasure and pride to relatively uninvolved parents. On the other hand, a strong-willed, irritable, and unpredictable child can drive the best of parents crazy. Many times the success or failure of guiding a child through the challenges of adolescence depends more on how good of a fit the parent and child are for each other.

Much like romantic partnerships, parents and children need a level of compatibility to work well together. Sometimes it takes a great deal of work to get the pulse of your child in sync with your own. It might be easier if parents and children existed in isolation, but there are other dynamic influences to consider: the relationships with siblings, the relationship with the same-sex parent as well as the opposite-sex parent, the possibility of growing up in a blended family, and the ever-developing relationships that exist outside of the home. Put all of these together and you have the makings of a complex network of relational experiences that shape the child's understanding of his environment and subsequently his understanding of how to achieve pleasure and avoid pain.

In addition, each life experience has a profound impact on our pulse. These life experiences include our success or failure in meeting developmental milestones, our socioeconomic status, the cultural climate of our neighborhood, our performance in school, our experiences with the opposite sex, and any sudden or unpredictable changes in our lives (moves, job or school transfers, traumatic events, or awards, for example). These experiences test and shape our frustration tolerance, our moral values, our personal preferences, our sensitivities, our attraction to others, and our virtues and vices. It is important to realize that your own pulse as a parent will be shaped by your personality and the experiences you have with your children. Be open to this.

Checking Your Teenager's Pulse

Most people don't feel their blood pulsing through their bodies unless they consciously check it. The same is true for the unspoken rules by which we live our lives. We don't realize how much they control us until we become conscious of them. This control happens in the form of a self-fulfilling prophecy. Much of the work of talk therapy is in getting clients to understand how their past experiences generate their present perceptions, which in turn determine their future actions and outcomes.

For example, if I was shamed early in life by authority figures who told me I was no good, I am more likely to expect shaming from other current authority figures. As a result, I might choose to avoid attending church, work functions, or other social gatherings where authority figures are present for fear of facing that "inevitable" shame. My avoidance, however, generates further disconnection, distrust, and unworthiness. Hence, it becomes a self-fulfilling prophecy. I told myself I was shameful and worthy of being alone, and my actions make me so.

Let's say, however, that despite my shame I take a risk and choose to be social. If I am still unaware of the influences of my past, my sensitivity to shame might lead me to lash out in anger at the first sign of criticism in public. As a result, the people I've tried to engage shy away from me, afraid to offend me. Once again I find myself in the exact same situation: isolated and feeling shame because I believe that no one likes me.

This is where an individual's perception of an event is just as important as the event itself. For example, a woman who was sexually abused as a child will process sexual pleasure differently than a woman whose sexual identity developed in the context of a nurturing and protective family of origin. A woman who grew up in a high-pressure, first-world society that values outward appearances of perfection and control will process the pleasures of a delicious meal differently from an individual who grew up in a third world country where food was scarce. Conscious awareness of our basic tendencies, given our genetics and our experience of the world, is the only way we can begin to change the direction of our lives. If you want to resurrect your teenage zombie, you must first check his pulse, which is comprised of the influences that direct his decisions. You must also be willing to consider how your own pulse as a parent has served to create a unique dynamic between you and your adolescent. You may need to consider changing that dynamic moving forward. This is tough work. Many people need family therapy in order to break these bonds and reform them. Are you willing to take drastic measures? Remember, this is a zombie apocalypse. You can survive it, but you have to understand it first.

The teenager who has a healthy pulse is not necessarily the teenager who comes from a perfect family or has made all the right choices along the path to adulthood. The teenager who develops a healthy pulse is the teenager who has an overarching belief system that rationally explains the events of his life, pleasurable or painful. This clarity provides a road map for how to respond to his circumstances and make wise decisions moving forward with the proverbial cards he has been dealt.

Instilling the Framework for a Healthy Pulse

How can you know that you are being successful in life if you have no measurement for success? How can you know that you are accomplishing the purpose for which you were created if it hasn't been outlined for you? Having a pulse helps us to feel safe in a large and dangerous world filled with an infinite number of choices that can bring us either pleasure or pain. The goal is for your child to get to the end of his life, not devoid of pain, but with the sense of satisfaction that life was worth living. This is a daunting task, because most teenagers don't think much about the future. They live for the moment and don't often process the reality of future goals and achievements. However, with ongoing education, experience, and persistence on your part, a pulse will be generated within your teenager that will revitalize his life and lead to a great future. The following elements are required to generate a healthy pulse.

A Healthy Pulse Requires a Clear Outline of Rules and Expectations

Too many parents create rules on the fly for their own convenience, enforcing them at times and reneging on them at other times based solely on how the parent feels in the moment. This is a surefire way to enrage a zombie teenager. There is nothing worse than feeling like you are tiptoeing through a minefield, not knowing if you will get what you want or be blasted for asking. The parents who are clear and consistent will avoid many unintended explosions between them and their teenagers. Creating an operating system within the family with very clear rules—such as curfews, financial limits, and privileges—that are based on a trusting relationship give a solid context by which adolescents can think through their own decisions. This context is much safer for their development than the harsh reality of the outside world. Your child may not be able to grasp the long-term effects recreational drugs will have on their brain in twenty years, but they do get that smoking cigarettes results in being grounded for the next month. The older your adolescent gets, the more experiences he or he will have had to help solidify the framework by which he lives his life.

A Healthy Pulse Requires Flexibility

Most psychologists would agree that two extreme forms of parenting can have a negative impact on a child. The very rigid authoritarian parenting focuses on following rules without question. Children are expected to obey simply because they are the child and their parents are the adults. On the other hand, permissive or uninvolved parenting has no rules or boundaries. Children are left to decide for themselves how to fulfill their desires. In either extreme, children tend to lack a healthy pulse: the first group because they are never allowed to make decisions and the second group because they are never taught how.

The most effective form of parenting is called authoritative parenting. This form of parenting provides a healthy level of control and structure while also providing continual explanations for the purpose behind the rules and expectations. It also allows for some level of flexibility for a child to choose. It is essential that parents allow their children to have some say in the overarching rules and regulations of the family structure.

The fight for independence is one of the chief struggles your children face at this stage in life, and rightly or wrongly, they may see you as an obstacle to that independence. They may refuse your advice purely on the principle that "I'm old enough to make my own decisions." They do not want to feel controlled or limited, but they fail to recognize the responsibilities that go along with their newfound freedom. Many parents worry that to be flexible in the face of such pressure will eventually lead to a caving or falling apart of order. The saying goes, "If you give them an inch, they will take a mile." However, if you have successfully established the rules, you can then decide if the situation at hand warrants leniency. This should involve an intentional sit-down conversation with your teenager to discuss what makes this situation worthy of your flexing the rules or expectations. If leniency is granted, it should also be clearly stated that for future incidences the rule/expectation still stands.

Giving your teenager a voice in the establishment of rules and expectations encourages him to have skin in the game. If he has been a part of the decision-making process used to establish the pulse between you, he is less likely to argue when you turn up the pressure on his behavior.

Flexibility also allows you the ability to listen to a teenager's viewpoint without having to make an immediate decision. During intense conflict, any amount of wiggle room you have to postpone a final decision helps to ease tensions and ensure that rules are enforced with as little emotion as possible. The best phrase you should incorporate into your conversations with your teenager is, "I need some time to think about that." It is better to be flexible and postpone a decision than to have a rigid, blanket stance on issues that might be negotiable. Rigidity is the best way to lose credibility with your teenager when you find yourself backpedaling on rules that have backfired on you, because they turned out to be unenforceable or destructive.

Third, being flexible establishes a stronger precedent on the nonnegotiable and actually helps you to avoid arguments on those subjects that are most important to you. If you become a parent who says yes as often as possible, your children will know that you mean business when you say no. This follows the tried and true adage of "Choose your battles wisely."

Finally, flexibility allows you the option of letting your child suffer from the natural consequences of his decisions. This in turn may save you from having to be the adversary in every troublesome situation. This will also help to enhance your credibility in situations where your teenager comes back, having suffered the natural consequences of his decisions, and is willing to admit that you were right after all.

Being able to flex a bit is called "grace." When you provide grace to your teenager, it allows him to see that your actions are well thought out and that you are ultimately acting with his good in mind.

A Healthy Pulse Must Have an Attainable Connection Between Point A and Point B

Think about the way the circulatory system works. The further the vessels are away from the heart, the weaker the pulse. If your teenager doesn't see the point of your rules, his drive and motivation to follow them is going to be very weak. If teenagers do not believe in the goals they are being driven toward—either that they are worthwhile or that they are achievable—good luck trying to discipline them. Some parents' expectations are so unreasonable or strict that they stifle any drive inherent within their children. Others' goals are so far out in the future that their teenagers cannot catch the vision, so they quickly lose sight of what is important. Setting attainable goals and using these goals to pull zombie teenagers forward will keep them headed in the direction you envisioned for them. For example, Brent was trying to teach his son the importance of saving for the future. Instead of using a good college education as the goal to be achieved— something his fifteen-year-old son wasn't even sure he wanted at the time—Brent used the incentive of a new car. The reward of a new car was a more immediate, attainable goal for his son to pursue and still accomplished the more lasting character trait of fiscal responsibility.

A Healthy Pulse Requires Constant Maintenance

Life can be brutal. Teenagers get pretty beat up by the challenges that life throws at them. Physically, when someone gets smacked in the arm, a bruise will form. A bruise is evidence of a broken blood vessel that needs repairing. Your teenager's pulse will only stay strong if in moments of failure, you and your teenager stay on track and stop the bleeding of mindless reactivity to hurts and discouragements along the path to success. Know that scars will form, depending on the severity of the injury, but the pulse can remain intact if you act quickly and appropriately to provide discipline, love, understanding, and grace. Expect your child to choose unwisely. Expect him to fall and get hurt. But keep an ongoing dialogue and incorporate the principles above to ensure that the bumps, cuts, and bruises of life don't lead to a bleeding out.

The Dangers of a Pulse-less Life

Entropy is a law of physics that states that when there is no external source of power or control, systems gradually fall into disorder and decay. In life there are seven universal pleasures we hope to obtain and seven universal pains we wish to avoid. What we want is justice, acceptance, connection, accumulation of material possessions, comfort, success, and physical health. What we seek to avoid is injustice, rejection, loneliness, loss of material possessions, painful discipline, failure, and physical death.[1] What is interesting when we consider these two lists is this: the universal pleasures listed are never guarantees, but the universal pains are. Pleasure is not a right for human beings. We have to work for it. Pain, however, can be passively experienced. If we sit back and allow people to take advantage of us, they will. If we do not work to connect with people, we will face rejection and loneliness. If we do not work at maintaining the material possessions we have, we will lose them. If we fail to pay our taxes, we will be disciplined by the IRS. If we do not persevere on a challenging task, we will fail to complete it. If we do not maintain our health, we will die. Our pulse for life keeps us on track toward our goals, even when the pain is strong.

Zombies demand immediate pleasure. They are either unwilling or incapable of enduring pain. Their lust for life, depicted in the movies by their thirst for blood, leads them to act without constraint, settling for immediate pleasures at the cost of wreaking havoc on all around them. A real-life example is the individual struggling with an addiction. Video games, drugs, alcohol, gambling, sex, food, shopping, and other such pleasures become immediate ways to feel good in the moment, but the long-term sacrifices are great: poor health, lack of education, limited job opportunities, drained finances, broken relationships, guilt, shame, and even death.

The effects of addiction are an example of what can happen to someone who lives a pulse-less life. Addiction, whether chemical or behavioral, has a clear biological component that affects an addict's brain. Alcoholics Anonymous calls it a "physical bankruptcy."[2] The more we study addiction, the more we understand that genetic factors can predispose someone to it. In addition, repeated exposures to the addictive substances or behaviors also serve to change the basic structure and functioning of the brain, making it very difficult to maintain a healthy life pulse.

Despite these physical changes, however, Alcoholics Anonymous also describes a "moral and spiritual bankruptcy"[3] within an addict. They have developed a belief system around the addictive experience that they use to justify destructive behaviors. This belief system must be changed in order for the addict to maintain sobriety.[4] He must restore a healthy pulse, a newly structured way of thinking, feeling, and behaving. Many addicts and alcoholics have adopted the twelve-step model of recovery as their pulse for living life. Your goal as a parent of an adolescent zombie is to help establish a similar kind of pulse for the challenges your child will face in his life.

Maintaining Your Own Pulse as a Parent

When faced with a zombie's pulse-less pursuit of its passions, many parents run. Because of the aggressive or manipulative tendencies zombies display during their pursuit of pleasure at the cost of others, most people are disgusted and repulsed by them. A parent's tendency to distance themselves emotionally from zombie adolescents is understandable. We all want to protect ourselves from ongoing abuse. One parent, in response to his son's verbal assault during a family meal, said, "I don't even want to see your face." The rift that occurs as a result of interactions like this can last for years. Bitterness, resentment, and defensiveness come between the zombie and his family, leading him to feel more shame and engage in further self-destructive behaviors used to dampen the pain of more broken relationships.

Unfortunately, your own desire for peace and pleasure may lead you to throw up your hands in disgust and cease all interactions with your adolescent. Though you might never tell anyone, you've longed for that do-over. In your weaker moments of fantasy, you've contemplated disowning him (not seriously of course—the orphanage said he was too old anyway).

In all seriousness, parents are human too. Some respond to their children's outbursts in kind, allowing their own abusive language to poison their interactions with their kids. Others escape from under the pressure of constant conflict by using drugs or alcohol. Some parents just release all boundaries and hope that the child and the rest of the family survive long enough for the zombie to wander away. You have to fight these urges to escape into unhealthy and destructive patterns. Just as you are working to establish within your adolescent a pulse or framework for pursuing pleasure and avoiding pain, you must find healthy outlets for dealing with the intense emotions you are also feeling as you engage the zombie in your home.

Practice what Aristotle called the "golden mean of virtue" and learn to respond "at the right time, about the right things, toward the right people, for the right end, and in the right way."[5] This is the essence of a healthy pulse. We all face pain and suffering in our dealings with our kids. The goal is to respond in a healthy way to those hurts, in a way that brings closer connections in relationships rather than distance and isolation, more productivity in our work rather than destruction, and greater pleasures in our lives rather than despair. The following story is an example of how a couple chose to maintain their pulse with a very difficult teenage zombie, and in the end they saw the reward for their perseverance.

Jack came to my office because he was failing in school. He spent hours playing video games late into the night and then would sleep through classes the following day. He claimed that school was boring and he didn't see the point. He had started smoking marijuana with a group of friends and would sneak out of the house regularly in the middle of the night just to "hang out." His parents reported having no idea what to do and were frightened that Jack was going to flunk out, get in trouble with the law, or even worse, harm himself physically.

Because there were several concerns with Jack, including his poor performance in school, his addictions to video games and marijuana, his poor choice of friends, and his lack of self-care evidenced by his staying out late and not sleeping, I could totally understand why his parents were overwhelmed. But I started with Jack where I start with most kids. What was motivating him?

> **David:** You mentioned that school was boring and you didn't see the point. Can you explain that to me a little further?
>
> **Jack:** Yeah, I just don't see how studying world geography or algebra is going to help me in life. My plan is to become a computer programmer and make video games. I don't need these other subjects to do that. These guys in the gaming industry make tons of money, and most of them didn't even go to college.

I wasn't about to engage Jack in a debate over the validity of his statements. His parents had already attempted that, spending hours lecturing and arguing with him over the irrationality of his beliefs about college and the gaming industry. They had done a great deal of research, in fact, to determine what was required in order for Jack to pursue his dream of being a programmer. They tried to show him the evidence, but he just ignored it.

Instead, I chose to focus on his present motivations, exploring what his video games, marijuana, and friendships provided for him that school did not.

> **David:** Tell me about marijuana. What do you like about it? (Jack was visibly taken off guard by the question. He was used to being lectured on the negative effects of marijuana and had never had anyone show an interest in what it did for him.)
>
> **Jack:** Well, it mellows me out. I don't have to think about anything important. The world seems calm

and peaceful. I feel more connected with my friends when I'm on it, and I just feel good overall. (His answers to the same question about video gaming and hanging out with friends were similar; they made him feel good, accepted, accomplished, and important.)

David: Do you see any downside at all to any of these behaviors?

Jack: (Whether he did or not, his answer was typical of many teenage zombies.) Not really. I don't understand why my parents can't just let me live my life the way I want to. I mean, I'm not hurting anyone, and the whole school thing isn't that big of a deal. I can figure all that out later.

Jack had all the rewards without any foreseeable pain, so how could I blame him for the choices he was making? Sometimes therapy can start with education, but I could have sat with Jack all day, as his parents had before, and lectured him about the potential consequences of his behaviors, and that would have meant nothing to him. I might have extolled the virtues of a healthy work ethic, daily exercise, a sober mind, and honoring his parents. I could have told him how morally wrong he was for dishonoring his parents' hard work in raising him. It would have been all wasted breath. Jack was living for the moment and trusting that everything in the future would work itself out. He was a zombie who needed experience in, not lectures about, true life.

This is where I turned to his parents for help. Fortunately, Jack was open to their involvement in therapy, and he signed a release allowing them to participate. If Jack had refused, I might have continued to work with him for a while, attempting some level of education and encouragement, but I certainly could not have forced him to do anything he did not want to do.

Some of you parents, in reading that, might think, *Ha! Shows how little you care, Dr. Henderson. You might be able to admit defeat and give up like that, but I can't do that with my child that easily!* The truth is that acknowledging the futility of a situation and doing less is actually not giving up. Sometimes it is the best offense. You will see that this is exactly what Jack's parents did.

In considering Jack's failure to perceive any negative consequences for his behavior, his parents and I explored some solutions that would give him a taste of the real world. What motivated Jack more than friends, marijuana, and video games? You guessed it: food, shelter, and clothing. When in doubt, start with the basics.

Jack's parents purchased padlocks for their pantry and refrigerator. They adopted that old proverb "He who does not work shall not eat." Jack had no money of his own because he did not have a job. He ate well as a result of the goodness and graciousness of his parents. Not anymore. If Jack wanted to eat with the rest of the family, he had to demonstrate that he had done his schoolwork as well as several other agreed-upon chores around the house. Otherwise, he was allowed to fix his own meals at designated times and with limited healthy ingredients. If Jack's clothes smelled like marijuana, his mother threw them in a sealed bin for him to wash himself. Jack's video games and television mysteriously disappeared. Jack was welcome to break curfew, but because his parents changed the locks and installed a security system, he had to stay out if his parents went to bed.

For a while, Jack resisted these changes. He spent the night at his friends' houses. They, of course, were very understanding and sympathetic—for a while. But Jack's mooching eventually got on their nerves too, and they stopped answering his calls and knocks at their doors. Eventually, Jack decided to play ball with his parents. The future pain, which he had little concern over before, became very real to him in the present.

Now his parents had to address their own motivations in choosing to make or not make some of these drastic changes. They had to face the pain of being labeled cruel, uncaring parents. They had to accept the possibility that none of their efforts would succeed and that Jack really would do something to hurt himself. They had to be willing to give up their hope of having a successful son who would one day make them proud. Ultimately, they had to choose their motivation for action. This required honesty and openness about the needs they wanted their child to meet. You, too, have to be honest about your motivations.

What If I've Already Messed Up?

If you are feeling discouraged by your child's lack of pulse and you are blaming yourself for his struggles, realize that every parent has regrets. The influence you could have had in the past can still be corrected in the present. You can start now by helping to create new emotional memories that will be hardwired into your child's brain for future reference when he enters adulthood. To do this, however, you must develop three important qualities within yourself: intentionality, consistency, and empathy. You will notice that each one of these traits corresponds to the pulse we are trying to generate within our kids.

Intentionality involves a conscious awareness of our motivation. When we act intentionally, we act with purpose. This is exactly what we want from our teenagers: "Think about what you are about to say or do," we tell them. But it is not enough just to say it; we have to model this behavior for them as well. If we want our kids to be aware of the spark within them, we have to show them how to find it. This isn't easy. Past memories of frightening or anger-inducing events can spark us to act without thinking. Sometimes we lash out in anger, fear, or despair, just like our kids do. But if we can keep in mind that every interaction with our child is an opportunity to create a new memory that will have an emotional impact on his future, we will recognize the value of intentionality.

There are many behavioral techniques to help with this. Although cliché, counting to ten really does work. It gives us just enough of a buffer to think about what we want to say or do next. Sometimes repeating a person's statements or questions not only helps us to be clear on what he is communicating, but also gives us a pause to think about the situation. Be slow to speak and quick to listen. Time-outs may be important. Write down your thoughts on paper before you state them. Set a timer to allow each person to speak equally without interruption.

One way to be intentional is to share our own experiences in times of relative tranquility and peace. Too often we wait until a crisis arises and then try to pound truth into a mind that is consumed by overwhelming emotions. In some respects, we have lost the art of storytelling in our society. We have allowed Hollywood to take over this art form, and in doing so, we have sacrificed control over the messages that shape our children's understanding and experience of the world. Take time to communicate the principles of life regularly to your teenager without any pretense or immediate agenda; this will have a more profound effect on his attitude and actions than lectures after a failure or during a crisis.

Communicating with younger teenagers may require you to develop traditions around dinnertime instead of the grab-and-go meals most modern families are accustomed to. For older teens you may have to schedule weekly coffee appointments just to catch up. Avoid lecturing. Share your life with them. Talk about the challenges of your day and how you handled them. Get their perspective too. Treat them like adults, and they will grow into the role naturally.

At other times we must intentionally step back and let our children experience some of the consequences for their actions alone. The expression "Next time, you'll think twice about your actions," implies that they have had a first-time experience to draw upon. Whatever it takes, model intentionality and your kids will learn from you what it means to act with purpose.

Consistency creates routine, routine builds structure, and structure contains pulse. Consistency is important because humans learn by repetition. The more often you model a certain behavior for your children, the more likely it is to be remembered, expected, and adopted. This is true of all forms of learning: exercise, studying, performing, and socio-emotional intelligence. To be consistent, we must realize that there are some things we can control and some things we cannot.

What we cannot directly control are our own or our teenagers' emotions and physiological reactions to those emotions. They come and go depending on the situation. They may even be different in the same situation. For example, your child's giddy joking at the dinner table might amuse you one evening and annoy you the next. The behavior hasn't changed, but your emotions have. Some days you feel good and some days you just feel bad. This is normal. Your teenager is the same way. On some occasions, he may be open to your advice. On other days, he may argue with everything you say. This too is normal.

Emotions are not bad. We need emotions just as much as we need logic to act effectively. Your limbic system, the emotional center of your brain, is not an obsolete part of your "evolved" brain that your cortex, the rational decision-making part of your brain, must simply deal with. No, it is extremely important and should be listened to, not suppressed. Problems arise when we fail to evaluate our emotional reactions to situations and respond consistently (and appropriately). We cannot directly control our emotions, but we can directly control our thoughts and our reactions to them. The more consistent you are in this endeavor, the clearer the framework you create for your teenager to interact with. If your responses to anger, sadness, or fear are unpredictable, your children will never learn how to respond appropriately to your feelings. In fact, we use the phrase "walking on eggshells" to describe the angst we feel when dealing with a person who is inconsistent in their responses. If you want your kids to be clear on your expectations for their lives, then you must be consistent with them and repeatedly respond in healthy ways to their behavior.

Finally, empathy is essential to encourage a healthy pulse within your son or daughter. Understanding the brain differences we discussed previously allows us to approach our adolescents in several ways. One is simply to allow for more patience with them as they mature into fully grown adults. Empathy can go a long way in fostering healthy relationships with our children during stressful times. Sometimes we interpret our children's actions as blatant defiance of our authority, when in reality they are acting without thinking. We take personal offense to actions that may be a normal part of human development. We must also understand that the adolescent brain does not have the same wealth of experience to draw on when making decisions. Their brains have not had the chance to formulate as many memories, giving them a more accurate intuitive sense.

The harder you work to understand the struggles your teenager is facing, the better equipped you will be to strengthen him by providing the healthiest balance of encouragement and challenge. Empathy is the ability to put yourself in someone else's shoes. It is not, "What would I do if I was in their situation?" but rather "What is it like to be them in their situation?" Try to understand their personality and experience, get into their brains so to speak, and really understand them. Coaches sometimes try to do this by having their players take psychological tests. They want to understand how hard they can push their players and what kinds of interactions, incentives, and impositions are most likely to motivate them. The same can be said for your relationship with your child. If you don't understand him, how can you possibly expect to motivate him?

Understanding your child is easier said than done. The reason is that it is hard to set aside our own thoughts, emotions, and judgments to look at a situation objectively when so much is at stake. If you cannot empathize with your teenager's struggles, it might be helpful to get an outside opinion from a friend, adviser, or counselor. Asking yourself what you're missing is not a sign of weakness but a sign of pulse in your own character that says, *I am willing to be teachable and explore new ideas in order to overcome the challenges that exist between me and my child.* When your child sees how hard you are working to understand his experience of life, you will gain credibility in his eyes. Your child will be more likely to comply with your guidance, knowing that you have done the hard work ahead of time to understand him.

With these three qualities, you can actually make changes in your teenager's hardwiring, even at this stage of development. In fact, more and more studies are being performed on the power of cognitive and behavioral interactions between people to change thoughts, emotions, behavior, and possibly even brain structure and functioning. Remembering how the brain organizes and uses emotional memories will help you to stay intentional, consistent, and empathetic with your teenage zombie. With time, your behavior will serve to resurrect the pulse he needs to return to the land of the living.

Strategy Questions

1. What are the boundaries that you have established within your family? Where are you experiencing pushback on these boundaries from your zombie teenager? On a scale of one to ten, how effective are you at keeping your teenager in line?
2. What changes in your own personal pulse might be helpful to become more efficient and effective at channeling your teenager's passions? Be as specific as possible.

CHAPTER 12

The Fiber of Life: Determination

Lyle, one of the many teens I've seen in my clinical practice, had always been a compliant kid at home and a good student. He was handsome, naturally introverted, and kept to himself often, though he did have a small set of close friends. His parents never suspected that a zombie was lurking beneath his unassuming exterior. They would have told you he was the perfect son until, suddenly (it seemed), he started spending hours each day isolating in his room. His grades began to suffer, he was in constant conflict with his parents over the household rules, and he argued consistently with his siblings over chores. His motivation for anything he used to enjoy had waned, and he was gaining weight at a staggering rate. His parents, frustrated and confused by his behavior, tried lecturing him, scolding him, even pleading with him, but their words fell on undead ears.

After several therapy sessions, it became apparent that, prior to his decline, Lyle had taken a risk and asked a female classmate to the prom, only to be rejected outright. He had spent months talking to her, trying to impress her with his intelligence and humor. He had worked hard to make her like him. Later he found out from a friend that the girl had referred to him as a loser and said she would not have wanted to be caught dead with him. The blow to his identity was shattering, but he didn't tell his parents. He tried to pretend nothing had happened. With such a rejection, however, there was no wondering why he chose to escape into the quiet solitude of his room, where he continued to be master of his environment. It was the first time he was confronted with the reality that he could not guarantee acceptance from another person, even if he did everything perfectly.

After the rejection, Lyle tried several times to break free from the thickening shell of apathy that surrounded him, but his sensitivity to further rejection from others left him wounded, shaken, and discouraged. He worried constantly over what others were really thinking of him. He found that he couldn't trust anyone's stated feelings. He knew deep down that they thought he wasn't good enough. His sense of failure relationally left him feeling powerless and discouraged in other areas of his life, such as academics, extracurricular activities, and family responsibilities. When he came to see me, he was floundering and his family was scared to death of the zombie he had become.

Through the therapy process, Lyle and I began talking about his pain. He began to see that, in all of his relationships, he had created an aura that he had it all together. This initially attracted people, but deep down it failed to give him the sense of security and confidence he longed for. It also didn't provide the kind of acceptance from others he really wanted. The more people told him how much they liked him, how much they enjoyed being with him, how talented and smart he was, the less he believed them.

Though he was scared, Lyle and I began to talk about what it would be like to live more transparently, showing people some of the bad and the ugly in addition to the good. We began to work toward accepting some of his shortcomings, his quirks and eccentricities, and even his limitations. We processed the inevitable losses and rejections that might come as a result of exposing people to these parts of himself, but we also considered the greater rewards that might come: a deeper trust in the people who knew and accepted the real him, the help he could receive from admitting weaknesses, and the potential surprises that might come from having one door shut and another opened.

We never found out the real reason why the girl he asked to the prom rejected him, but he soon came to see that it did not matter. If working so hard to be perfect still resulted in such pain, he decided that it was time to live differently. This was the moment at which new life started for him. He began to develop the fiber necessary to accept rejection as an inevitable part of being real and transparent.

As he progressed in therapy, he developed a clearer awareness of his tendency, in the face of rejection, either to work harder to hide his insecurities and flaws or to retreat into isolation when he felt unable to keep up the masquerade. These all-or-nothing reactions occurred with his family, his friends, and teachers.

With practice, he started taking more initiative, practicing transparency, verbalizing his needs, and accepting others' responses to those needs, positive or negative. He began to see himself not as a loser, but as someone with value despite his very real flaws, someone with work to do on himself but good enough to accept himself in the process of growth and change. He was someone with a right to his own views and opinions, agreeable or disagreeable, no matter how others treated him. This change in mind-set initially generated more conflict with his parents, who were not used to his transparency and saw his assertiveness as defiance, but as they increased their communication with him and took time to listen and be responsive, they felt more at ease with his taking charge of his life. As a result, they trusted him more and gave him greater ownership of his duties and responsibilities. They began to treat him more like an adult, and he responded well to it. He shifted from discouragement to encouragement, which boosted his confidence, increased his productivity, decreased his need to escape into video games, and eventually led to deeper connections with people inside and outside his family. Lyle grew stronger in these areas only because he was willing to face the pain of his imperfections and accept them, even as he sought to change them.

Looks Can Be Deceiving

The Lyle that first presented to my office is an example of the third and final type of teenage zombie. Though they may have the spark of life and an established pulse, they lack one essential element: fiber. Fiber represents the determination and confidence a teenager needs to sit with uncomfortable emotions or situations. The most uncomfortable situation for a teenage zombie without fiber is failure.

Teenagers who lack fiber may outwardly appear to be put together. They may even be successful at pursuing goals like homework, sports, jobs, and hobbies. Outwardly, they may appear to get along with others. They are pretty compliant with your rules and expectations. All of this is great except for one problem—their fiber is weak because it is held together by their fear of failure, not their love of life.

Lyle's story illustrates the fact that although fiber-less zombies may not do anything outwardly wrong or deviant, they are tortured internally. Lyle's parents had no idea he was struggling early on because he was able to hide the pain, but he needed permission to let go of the façade of perfection and accept his failures as much as his successes. Many driven adolescents, ones who are outwardly successful, struggle with anxious conditions that are hard to observe from the outside. Often they are the firstborns, the quiet ones, the responsible ones, the compliant ones. Parents feel safe with them and even cater to them, but they may also be harder on them, have higher expectations of them, and assume they can handle everything because they rarely see the growing beast inside of them. The child is too scared to reveal it.

These adolescents are classically people pleasers. They seek approval from their parents and others in authority. They are very disciplined and motivated to succeed. They have what many would call type A personalities. These zombies need to face their weaknesses, accept their shortcomings, and let down their guard in order to find strength. Instead of hiding the spirit of the beast within, they need to let it come out.

Life gets pretty scary when we start believing that our material and relational needs will be satisfied only if we maintain an illusion of perfection. We start to lose hope in life if we believe that smaller failures are proofs of a greater, ultimate failure lurking within us. If a fiber-less teenager has any experience that leads her to doubt her ability to achieve success in the business district or the public square—she does not get the grade she wanted on a test, the girl he asks to the prom rejects him, a parent gets angry with her—she or he falls apart. This is because deep down inside, despite all of their other outward successes in life, these teenagers do not possess the fiber necessary to achieve the one success necessary for their survival: the determination to be gracious to themselves and others in the face of human limitations and failures.

It may sound paradoxical to say we must fail well to be successful, but it is true. I've heard people say, "I will never accept failure. It's not an option." They are correct in one sense. Failure is not an option; it is inevitable. What they really mean to say is, "I will not allow failures to stop me from living a successful life." In this respect, they possess the determination or fiber needed to overcome discouragement, learn from their mistakes, and change their course if necessary. If we cannot write failure into the story of our lives, our identity will always remain fragile. It will change constantly with the ebb and flow of our circumstances rather than remaining constant and secure in the face of challenges.

To be truly happy in life, we must accept that we have inherent value, even with our flaws and failings. A fiber-less teenager doesn't accept this. They can't yet see that weaknesses are as important, if not more important, than our strengths in guiding us toward the true source of abundant life, love itself.

Think about it: if I were perfect in and of myself, I would have no need for relationships. But if I accept that I am incomplete, unfinished, or unfulfilled, I will be open to receiving that which will satisfy my deepest longings and needs. For many, God, the Creator of love and life, is the ultimate source of this completion. Sarah Young, author of *Jesus Calling*, says that our confidence comes from the knowledge that we are complete in Him.[1] But God also uses people to provide evidence of His love and acceptance of us. To find such love and acceptance, we must be honest with ourselves and with others that we are lacking what we need on our own. Only then can we be provided for. And that which we have received, we can also give to others. Scripture says, "Love your neighbor as yourself."[2] To love your neighbor, you must love yourself. You must understand and accept the nature of who you really are, your strengths and weaknesses alike. This is the only way you can love and accept the complete nature of others as well. In the end, perfect love drives out all fear:[3] fear of rejection in the public square and fear of failure in the business district. This is what we strive for. This is what your teenager is striving for.

So how do we help our teenagers gain the fiber of a strong identity, to have confidence and determination in the midst of failure? There is no way around it: we must let them fail! You know as well as I do that this is easier said than done. None of us wants to see our children fail. But if we are overly motivated to prevent it, we have communicated implicitly to our kids that they will not be okay if they fail.

The method of resurrecting a zombie without fiber is counterintuitive to a loving parent's normal inclinations. It feels like I am saying, "Don't feel for your kids. Be emotionless and cruel and let them suffer." It's true: when we see our "good kids" struggling, we feel a natural affection for them and strongly desire to help them overcome. After all, they've earned it.

There is nothing wrong with this—to a point. However, if we believe that in every situation, there is a simple and effective solution that will fix all of our kids' problems, allowing them to advance quickly to the next level of achievement, we are wrong. Parents' typical gut reactions are to fight for a fiber-less zombie. They see their child suffering from anxiety and want to jump in with a quick but costly fix that will solve the problem. Usually parents feel successful at first. They offer solution after solution, each of which appears to take care of the problem for a time. They also do a tremendous amount of reassuring and emotional soothing. Talks lasting hours become circular. Like playing whack-a-mole, they help to suppress one fear only to find another one popping up. The beasts of anxiety and fear resurface with each new circumstance the adolescent feels ill-equipped to handle. The more the parent rescues, the weaker the teenager's fiber becomes. Each successive achievement comes with a deeper dread of a new and ensuing failure. In helping their children avoid failure, parents only make their children's sensitivity to it worse. The longer a teenager is prevented from failing, the harder failing successfully becomes. Over time the teenager begins to distrust others, believing that the only reason she is accepted is because of her performance. This distrust hardens a brittle shell, further distancing her from others who now feel intimidated by her seemingly perfect presence. This cycle continues to reinforce her fear of abandonment and her failure to find love and belonging. Parents, too, become emotionally exhausted and frustrated. They feel helpless, having become the only source of support and reassurance for their teenager.

This change in perspective and action is hard to accept for both adolescents and parents. A zombie without fiber looks to a parent to *reassure* her that everything in the future will be okay, *rescue* her from her problems, and *reinforce* her weaknesses with the parents' strengths so she will avoid failure and achieve success. Of course, this "help" does not get to the spirit of the problem. The problem is not failure itself. The problem is a fiberless zombie's inability to accept failure as a natural part of life.

If we are honest as parents, this is as much our problem as it is our teenagers'. We may tell our teenagers that we will love them no matter what, but let's face it: their failures are just as hard for us to accept. We feel disappointment. If it were possible to do, we would keep our kids from failure. None of us likes to see the ones we love in pain, and failure is painful. Unfortunately, if we do not consciously accept the impossibility of a life of uninterrupted successes, we are doomed to reinforce that illusion of such a life in the minds of our children.

For example, I met with a client and her mother, who was a professional dancer. My client was applying to colleges, looking to major in performance arts. She hoped to be accepted to a particular college, mainly because her mother and grandmother had both attended there. If accepted, she would keep the legacy going. In the session, Mom reassured her daughter that it would be perfectly fine if she did not ultimately get accepted to that college. "It's really not that big of a deal," she said. However, when I talked with Mom alone, she admitted that it would be devastating, not just to her daughter but to her as well. Her anxiety was palpable. If I could sense it, I was sure her daughter could sense it as well. Her body language, facial expressions, and behaviors betrayed her true feelings, despite her reassurances to the contrary. Mom was working just as hard, if not harder, to make sure her daughter got accepted.

Change came when Mom began to identify with her daughter's fears and be honest about them, not just with herself but with her daughter too. They processed together the difficulties of the potential failure, the reasons why they would both be disappointed, and what they could both do for each other and themselves if it did not work out the way they hoped it would.

Ironically, talking about the elephant between them did not worsen her daughter's anxiety as the mother had feared. It relieved it. The daughter's trust in her mother's assurances of love and acceptance increased, having experienced her mom's transparency and willingness to face the potential disappointments that might come. She was able to enjoy the application process more, putting her best foot forward during auditions without the dread of the final outcome that had plagued her before. In the end, she did not get accepted to the college she wanted, but having faced the potential failure and preparing emotionally for it beforehand, she was able to be content with the school that did accept her. Five years later, she is glad it didn't work out the way she had initially hoped. While at the school she attended, she happened to meet a professor who saw her potential and connected her with a famous studio in New York City where she has been performing and teaching ever since.

Dead Ears

In the face of failure, there is nothing wrong with affirming our teenagers with encouraging words. But there are times when these pep talks turn into arguments. Before parents realize it, they can find themselves in the middle of a heated debate. We try to assure our teenagers that they have not and will not fail. Rather than helping their children to accept their very real failures (past and present) and the probability of future failures as an important part of developing a strong identity, parents try to convince their children that they are smarter, better looking, or stronger than they really are. They make excuses for why a failure wasn't actually their child's fault or why it wasn't a valid assessment of her weaknesses or limitations. Parents avoid confronting what these limitations really mean for their child. This denial of the issue and refusal to consider the teenager's beliefs about herself, right or wrong, simply leads to more frustration on the part of the teenager. She will not believe your entreaties, even if what you are saying is true.

How many parents have heard a struggling teenager say, "You have to say that. You're my parent!" in response to their reassurances. Trying to reason with a teenager in this state can literally be like trying to stop a zombie that is attacking you. This is because any defense always creates an immediate state of war. You've set the stage for a debate you participate in rather than a performance you observe.

In the moment of crisis, it is better to accept your child's failure and explore what it means for her, rather than try to convince her that she really hasn't failed. The reason we debate with our teenagers, in part, is because we are anxious about what it will mean for their long-term identity if they believe they have failed. What if it is true? What if she really did fail? Do *you* believe she will be okay? Really?

Get Off the Stage

My encouragement to parents during an important event in their teenager's life is to envision their son or daughter on an imaginary stage. I ask them to picture what that stage looks like—is it set up for a political primary or a Broadway production? Then I ask them to picture where they, the parents, are standing. Are they at the opposing podium, ready to duke it out with words? Are they on set with their teenager, ready to fully immerse themselves in the drama about to unfold? Or are they off stage, in the audience, waiting to watch and write a review of what they see? My goal is to get parents off the stage completely. The only way to do this is for the parents to consider and reflect on their own emotional investment in the drama playing out. What is at stake for you, the parent, if the performance is a tragedy, a comedy, an epic adventure, or a horror show?

As difficult as it may be, parents need to separate their desires from their teenager's and become as unbiased an observer of their teenager's identity and actions as they can. It is okay to be moved emotionally by the performance, but you do not want to be a player in the show.

When the situational performance is over—that is, the test is passed or failed, the date says yes or no, the team wins or loses—the goal of the parent is not necessarily to communicate what she has observed about the quality of her child's outward performance. This is for the teenager to consider and comment on. The really important part of the performance for the parent is the epilogue or the closing monologue, so to speak. How does your teenager summarize the events that occurred, and how does she articulate her feelings about it? This is the part of the performance you can speak to, providing your observations and reflections. "I notice that you think you could have studied harder for the exam. How could that have been possible, given all your other responsibilities? It is interesting that you assumed this girl rejected you because you weren't funny enough. Is that the only possibility? I can hear your disappointment over the team's loss. I know you feel like you contributed to it. What is this going to mean for you at the next game?"

As your teenager responds, you keep observing and

reflecting. Feel free to insert your beliefs about the situation into the dialogue. It is every audience member's prerogative to have an opinion; just don't expect your teenager to agree with your opinions at first. It sounds strange, but the less emphasis you put on them believing your point of view, the more likely they are to accept it. You probably won't hear the "you have to say that; you're my parent" rebuttal, because you are turning ownership of their thoughts, feelings, and actions over to them. You are allowing them to see themselves the way they choose but also helping them to understand that their view of themselves may not be what others see. In the end, they have to own their identity and be comfortable with it. You cannot force it on them.

Let me explain further. If our identity is formed by the accumulation of experiences throughout life, then it is constantly changing. In that way, it is much like a story, a narrative that continues to play itself out until the final curtain call. Your teenager is telling this story internally with the thoughts and attitudes she chooses, and externally through her actions. Her emotions are what give the story passion and credibility. Every teenager has a script that determines the nature and direction of the narrative. She recites it to herself over and over again so that when it comes time for the performance, she can act it out with fluidity and unconscious ease. If her script says that she is martyr, she will act like a martyr and "kill" herself to please whatever audience she has. If her script says that she is the villain, she will invite hisses and boos by being antagonistic with everyone she meets. You can get a glimpse into anyone's script just by observing long enough. Watch the performance! You cannot do this if you are one of the players on stage. You have to step out of the situation as much as possible, emotionally, and be clear of what the performance is doing to you.

A client named John was telling me about a book he just finished, *Lone Survivor*. It's the story of a navy SEAL during the war in Afghanistan. Naturally, the conversation led to the unbelievable heroism of such men who risk their own lives for the safety and security of others. But then John made an interesting statement. He said, "Man, if that was me, I probably wouldn't have survived the hike into the mountains, let alone the firefight!" It was an innocent, humorous comment on the surface, but if you knew John, you would know that his script told him that he wasn't the survivor type. He wasn't even in the fight! He was a screwup, irrelevant, the guy who would trip on a rock and tumble off a cliff before getting to the battle.

The more I thought about it, the more I realized how much this script had defined John's identity and his subsequent experience of life. He had few hobbies and fewer friends. He had no serious romantic relationships. John was quintessentially "safe." There is nothing wrong with being safe, but John was not content in that safety. He wanted to take risks, but his script would not allow him to. The longer I met with him, the more I realized how, I, his therapist, was playing into his story. Each time we met, I found myself responding to his anxiety by working with him to improve his sense of safety and security. I found myself compelled to protect and reassure him, rather than challenge and confront him. In this way, I had become a player on the stage with him, rather than a member of the audience, witnessing the story he was living out on stage. It wasn't until I realized this and pointed it out to John that we changed the direction of the therapy.

In order to help, we decided to find one activity that he could pursue that had a modest level of risk but a tangible potential for reward. We settled on CrossFit. For those of you who do not know, CrossFit is an intense workout regimen, usually performed at a garage-like gym with a personal trainer and a team of other members. To do this, we had to consider the pain. For one, the cost was not cheap. A membership at a CrossFit gym is the equivalent of a monthly car payment. We also had to address all the what-ifs: What if I get hurt? What if I look stupid? What if I can't do the exercises? What if I don't see any changes? What if I can't fit it into my schedule? All of these questions fit with John's script and the "irrelevantly safe" character he tended to play.

Once we laid out all the contingencies, we turned the conversation to changing his script. Yes, all of these concerns were possibilities, but he would be the lone survivor. Others around him were going to fall, dropping out of the class. Not him. We talked about his concerns like they were bullets, flying all around him, sometimes breaking his skin, causing great pain, but he would be the lone survivor. The story would end with his triumph. At the end of the day, he was going to be stronger, physically and mentally, because of it.

Over the course of a year, there were many instances when John began talking and acting like an expendable, a sideliner. Each time, we changed the script, refocusing on the narrative, making it one of triumph and survival, not death and irrelevance. The transformation at the end of the year was stunning. He went from barely being able to do a pull-up to doing twenty-five in one set. This confidence carried over into his schooling and his relationships. He made some friends at the gym who invited him to hang out after the group sessions. Life for John became richer and more fulfilling, and it all started with the identity, the personae he chose to adopt.

As a parent, this is your role: the observer, the visionary, the narrator. You see for your teenager what she cannot see for herself and you speak it into her life, retelling her story from your perspective and letting her chose which version she would like to adopt. Give her experience and her identity a new label, one that fits more closely with true reality. Ideally, every positive experience would be incorporated by your teenager into a healthier and healthier identity, and every negative experience would be assimilated to fit that same healthy identity. Ultimately, it is the teenager's choice to decide what narrative to believe, but parents sometimes have to believe it for them first.

To do this, you must keep your identity separate from your child's. The more your identity depends on the identity of your child, the more undue pressure your child will feel to perform to a script written not by her, but by you. This will ultimately reinforce your sense of failure, discouragement, and helplessness. Much of our significance comes from our success or failure as parents. This is natural. But our significance should not rest solely on this. When our kids are struggling, we may have to stop and consider our own scripts. Are we thinking and acting like Dr. Frankenstein, regretting this creation we made? Are we the wicked stepmother from *Cinderella* or the absent and clueless father from *Hansel and Gretel*? Some parents have a fairy godmother complex, believing that they can fix every problem with a wave of their magic wand.

I cannot tell you what the right script is for you and your child. All I can do is encourage you to be aware of it and know how it is affecting your thoughts, your emotions, and your actions as they pertain to your child. A general rule of thumb, however, is that if you are trying to successfully launch your son or daughter into the world, your role as the parent should be diminishing further and further into the part of adviser, consultant, even friend. Remember, you're trying to step off the stage of the unfolding drama, bear witness to it, and provide a commentary on what you see. You cannot do this if you are one of the characters in the drama. At the end of the production, you should be applauding from the audience, not taking the last bow from the stage.

The Dangers of Rescuing a Fiber-less Teenager

Of course I do not mean that you should abandon your child. You can continue to be loving, supportive, and encouraging, but you must allow her to make her own decisions, even her own mistakes in life. She must learn to self-soothe, and the only way for this to happen is for you to step back, limit your contact, and let her flounder some. I know, it's easier said than done, but consider this: when someone is drowning, a lifeguard maintains her distance and offers a flotation device instead of a hand or an arm. If she must rescue the victim herself, she swims up behind the victim rather than approaching face-to-face. The reason for this is that a drowning victim will often grab onto his rescuer and pull her under the water with him, resulting in the death of two people, not just the possible death of one. You, as a rescuer, are no good to anyone if you suddenly find yourself drowning in your own emotions. You must believe in your adolescent. She has the intelligence and the moral framework for life. She just needs the courage to function independently. This has to involve courage in the face of failure and imperfection. You can be the impetus for that change if you are able to fight the urge to intervene and fix every problem she has.

Here are some truths to remember that will allow you to stay strong in the face of your child's fears and failures:

There Is a Limit to How Much Reassurance You Can Provide Your Child

As stated above, you can tell your child over and over again how much you believe in them, but if she does not believe in herself, no amount of reassurance on your part will save her from her insecurities. I often encourage parents with children who are never satisfied with the assurances of love, support, and faith given to them to turn it back on the child and ask, "What can I say to you that would help you to feel better?" Sometimes the child has an answer. At other times, she does not. Either way, it puts the responsibility on the child's shoulders to determine what kind of support she needs in the face of failure and discouragement. If she can come up with an answer, you as the parent then have the ability to decide if her request is reasonable or not. If not, you can explain why. It might infuriate your teenager at first. Perhaps she will become even more discouraged, but in the long run, it will be better for her because she will take ownership for the assurances she alone can provide herself.

There Is a Limit to the Amount of Rescuing You Can Do

Teenagers have the tendency to equate love with getting what they want. If you were really a good parent, you wouldn't deny them anything and everything they need for success, right? Wrong! It is okay to say no. Particularly in the face of failure. Who says you need to pay your zombie teenager's bail if she gets arrested for driving under the influence? Who says she needs the latest clothes so that she can impress her friends? Who says that when she forgets to do a homework assignment, you have to stay up with her all night and help her finish it? Of course, there is always a place for grace and mercy, but you have to decide if your actions are based in true love or fear. If you are acting out of fear, you are rescuing your child from the consequences of her behavior because you are worried about being the bad guy versus what will actually be best for her growth and independence. Acting out of love may be harder. The true sacrifice for you may be experiencing the pain of your child's suffering without intervening, even though it will be best for her in the long run. If you are not sure which direction to take, seek the counsel of those who have been there before.

There Is a Limit to How Much Reinforcement You Can Provide

You only have so many resources, material and emotional, at your disposal to reinforce your teenager's weaknesses. You may have more than one child to concern yourself with. If you are like most of us, your finances are limited. You only have so many connections. At some point, you have to say no. The same is true for the emotional energy you invest in a relationship. Parents can suffer from compassion fatigue. Trying to deal with a child's emotional ups and downs is exhausting. Parents start to feel guilty when, instead of providing encouragement and support, they get agitated and angry at their own inability to impart change. The rule of thumb to remember is that if you find yourself working harder than your teenager, you are working too hard. It is time to take a break, reexamine how much skin you have in the game, and accept your own limitations and failures when it comes to helping your children.

How to Challenge a Fiber-less Teenager

So far we have talked a lot about what we cannot do. Now that you have had a chance to face your own limitations and failures when it comes to your fiber-less teenager's struggles, you can begin to consider how you can effectively challenge your teenager. The best options are to make them aware of faulty thinking and encourage them to change their perspective.

What's the Real Fear?

The following is an example of an interchange I had with one of my clients. I think it helps to illustrate some of the actions you can take with your teenager as you confront common self-defeating thoughts that run through their minds in the face of failure. Here our approach with our zombie teenager needs to be directed at challenging her to confront the true nature of her fears, intellectually and experientially.

Then What? Challenging a Teenager to Unpack the Black Box of Fear

I spoke with a student named Molly who struggled with social anxiety and loneliness. She described an incident to me where she was listening to a group of fellow students talking about a topic she felt passionate about. When I asked why she did not join in, her response was, "I'm afraid it wouldn't make a difference. I'm not going to change anyone's opinion." This, on the surface, was Molly's specific fear of failure, but there was a deeper failure that scared her and needed to be unpacked. The following is a portion of our discussion:

David: "If you spoke and did not change anyone's opinion, what would that say about you?"

Molly: "I guess it would say that my ideas are stupid or unimportant to them or that I wasn't smart enough to get them to understand where I was coming from."

David: "So your motivation to remain silent in that moment was not because it was a pointless discussion or because you were not going to change someone's mind, but because you wanted to avoid a feeling of stupidity or unimportance. Is that correct?"

Molly: "Yeah, I guess it is."

David: "What would happen if they did think you were stupid?" (Then What?)

Molly: "I guess they would stop hanging out with me."

David: "And then what would happen?"

Molly: "Well, I would be alone. I would feel lonely and rejected."

David: "I can understand why that would be very painful for you. No one wants to be rejected or feel alone. But isn't that why you started seeing me in the first place? You were feeling alone and your anxiety was keeping you from making friends with people. In fact, you've felt alone for a long time because you've avoided people out of fear. What if you faced your fear? What would be the worst thing that could happen?" (Then what?)

Molly: "I would feel rejected and alone. I guess what I am already feeling. But at least if I don't say anything, no one will know that I actually deserve to be rejected and alone. They won't know how screwed up I really am."

Here was where we got to the deepest fear Molly had: her deepest fear was that she was not valuable, that she was worthless. That she had nothing to contribute. That she deserved to be alone, and that by interacting with people, it would prove her fears to herself and to the people with her.

Examine the Evidence

It is important, once you have identified the deepest fear of failure, to consider the evidence that proves or disproves the extent of the belief. Molly certainly had experienced rejection in the past. Because she was so quiet and introverted, she had experienced some bullying in her elementary and junior high years. But there was also evidence to suggest that when people really got to know her, she possessed qualities that made her likable and a good friend. This is what I wanted her to consider.

David: "Can you think of someone you know who you can talk to without worrying about changing their opinion or feeling smart or important? If so, why do you talk to them? Why do you let them know what you think or how you feel?"

Molly: "Well, I can talk easily to my best friend, Lauren. She understands me and does not judge me. I can tell her what I think or how I feel, and I know she will accept me for who I am."

David: "Do the two of you ever disagree?"

Molly: "Yes, but that doesn't matter. The disagreeing is part of what makes the conversation fun. We can let each other have our own opinions, and we learn from each other. We are motivated to understand where the other person is coming from."

David: "Then it sounds like the point of sharing with Lauren is not so you can change her mind, but so she can know you deeper and love you more fully as a person. Is that true?"

Molly: "Definitely. That's exactly it."

David: "It would seem to me that in order for you to have a friendship like that with Lauren, you had to start somewhere. You had to take a risk, right?

Molly: "I did, actually. I remember the first time I asked her to hang out at my place. I was so nervous it wasn't going to go well, but we had a great time. We just clicked for whatever reason."

David: "Tell me more about the reasons you clicked."

Molly: "Well, I guess to start, we had some similar interests. I really like to read and watch movies, and we enjoyed talking with each other about the stories, characters, and deeper meanings of the

ones we had both read or seen. But she was also
super encouraging. Anytime I told her something,
she seemed genuinely interested, and she built
up my confidence to talk more by asking more
questions." (Evidence that Molly's thoughts and
opinions are interesting, not unimportant, boring,
or stupid.)

David: "Sounds like Lauren saw some things in
you that she really liked. That, at least to her,
your ideas and opinions were not stupid or
unimportant?"

Molly: "Maybe. But I think she's just like that as a
person. She's super nice to everyone."

Here is where Molly wanted to retreat back to the script that
she tells herself. Lauren likes her, not because Molly is likable
or has value, but because Lauren is likable and has value. She
is just a nice person in general, so she has to be nice to Molly.
Molly wanted to tell herself that Lauren was hanging out with
her because Lauren is charitable. Lauren pities Molly.

At this moment, I felt tempted to debate with Molly, to
get up on stage at the opposing podium and try to force her
to accept that her belief was wrong. I wanted to argue because
I wanted her to see that she did have value. However, can you
see that if I had debated with her, I would have been communicating exactly what she believed about herself and what she
was trying, unconsciously, to get other people to affirm: namely,
that her opinions were stupid. *How can you think you don't have
value? That is so dumb!* In this way, I would be entering into the
drama playing out before me, rather than staying off the stage

as a member of the audience. Instead, I remained a part of the audience, watched the show unfold, and made her aware of this script she had written.

> **David:** "Looks and sounds to me like it's easier for you to believe that Lauren's hanging out with you just because she is a nice person, not because she sees things in you that draw her to you. Lauren must be an absolute saint, 'cause I don't know anyone who would hang out with someone as much as she hangs out with you just because she's trying to be nice."
>
> **Lauren** (laughing): "Well, she *is* a saint, but you're right. I know she values me as a friend. Sometimes I just don't know why. I feel so flawed as a person sometimes."

Now Molly is starting to consider the evidence that, at least in one relationship, she has been accepted and is valued. If we were to continue on this route, we might talk about other people in her life with whom she is close to further solidify the evidence that lots of people like her. However, we stuck with Lauren to get her to consider the *reasons* why she has value in this specific relationship. It appeared that she wasn't able or perhaps willing to see this.

Get a Second Opinion

Before a follow-up session, I asked Molly if she would be comfortable asking Lauren why she thought they were friends. She admitted that this might be embarrassing, but she was willing to give it a try. When she returned, she was able to articulate some of the qualities that Lauren had said Molly possessed—the things that made hanging out with Molly fun for Lauren. Of course, Molly still struggled to believe what Lauren had said.

> **David:** "Tell me what makes it hard for you to believe Lauren?"
>
> **Molly:** "Well, again, I feel like she is just being nice. I mean, I really believe that she thinks these things about me are true—that I'm funny, a deep thinker, caring, a good listener—but I feel like the longer she spends time with me, the more she is going to see my flaws and get tired of me or irritated with me."

Asking people for feedback about your performance, your strengths, and your weaknesses can be a very helpful way to get a clearer, more accurate picture of how people see you. However, a fiber-less zombie teenager can really struggle to accept the positivity because she knows deep down that she has a dark side that she is hiding. All the head knowledge in the world will not help to decrease her anxiety until she can have an experience where she lets the beast inside of her go a little bit and sees that it is okay.

Experiment

In Molly's case, I asked her to tell me what was some part of herself that she really wanted Lauren to see but was afraid of exposing. The point was not to make something up but to consider something that was really preventing their relationship from going deeper—something that was making Molly feel distant from Lauren, feeling unknown. Molly admitted that she struggled with anger and that this was a side of her that Lauren had never really been exposed to. Certain things Lauren did really irritated Molly, but she had always stuffed them down and not mentioned them because she didn't want to lose Lauren as a friend.

One of the most hurtful was that sometimes Lauren would tease her in front of other people. Molly knew that Lauren was not intentionally trying to be mean. In fact, Molly noticed that she did this with several of her close friends, but given Molly's past history of being bullied, it really hurt her and made her angry. During one of our sessions, we processed how she might talk out her anger with Lauren. We agreed that she would do it in a kind but firm way. We practiced what she would say and how Lauren might respond. Though she was very nervous about it, she took a chance and made Lauren aware of it.

To Molly's surprise, Lauren admitted that some of the teasing was because she felt jealous of Molly. Lauren felt intimidated by Molly's intelligence and ability to talk about deep ideas. Lauren had been trying to keep up with Molly in this area, but she felt insecure. Her teasing was a way of making her feel better. Lauren, in tears, asked Molly to forgive her.

Molly was shocked. She could not believe that Lauren could possibly find something about her to be jealous of, but even more shocking was that she was admitting it and asking for forgiveness. She said that the whole experience was overwhelming, but it made her feel even closer to Lauren as a friend. Molly's openness about her anger and sensitivity had led to Lauren's openness about her jealousy and teasing, the darker sides within

---

both of them, and they both provided grace and acceptance to each other in the end. Molly was beginning to see how being real about her faults and failures and showing some transparency actually strengthened her relationships and her confidence in herself that she had value to give another person. Her transparency and presence had made someone else grow.

Encouraging Risk

Molly was able to acknowledge that her relationship with Lauren was evidence that, despite her flaws, she had something of value to bring to the table. She still struggled with whether this could translate into other relationships with new people. She still had fears of rejection. In this way, she was acknowledging the downside of transparency—that rejection was still possible. To explore this, it was important to address the alternative: What was the pain that led her to seek out a relationship with Lauren in the first place?

> **David:** "So what pushed you to invite Lauren over to your place the first time?"
>
> **Molly:** "I knew something about her from observing her at school, and I really, really liked her. But that wasn't enough to get me to reach out to her. Basically, it came to the point that I was tired of spending my weekends alone. I was really lonely, and I guess asking her to hang out was worth the rejection if there was any chance of making a connection."
>
> **David:** "So, what you are telling me is the potential for a relationship with Lauren [the reward] was in

your mind both achievable and worth the risk of rejection [the pain], so you did it."

Molly: "That's it."

David: "I wonder if that risk is not worth the reward in some of these other relationships you have. As long as you keep that true desire in front of you, I think it would help motivate you to be more engaged socially and risk some of the pain you might face. It's not about changing other people's opinions or avoiding looking stupid or unimportant. It is about knowing and being known so that you can love and be loved deeply. That seems like a great thing to speak up for. What do you think?"

Molly: "That would be nice. But what if it never happens? What if I make all that effort and it doesn't produce the results I want?" (the fear)

David: "I hear you, and you are right. There is a lot of risk in living, but you have already demonstrated that the rewards are possible. Your relationship with Lauren proves that. You just have to keep that potential in mind. It might take time. You might get rejected by 90 percent of the people you reach out to. But on a scale of 1 to 100, that still would mean you have ten new friends you would not have had otherwise. That's the goal. You are here because you're tired of being alone, and I know your ultimate desire is to live in fellowship with other people. You just have to keep reminding yourself that the risk is worth the reward."

You see, deep down Molly knew what she really wanted. She wanted to have closer friendships, to feel known and accepted by the people in her life, and to overcome the loneliness and isolation she felt inside. In the moment, however, she lost sight of those goals and became motivated by her fears of rejection instead. She was afraid of her own limitations to achieve her goals. She was afraid that she would fail. But by hiding, she sank deeper into the pain she was trying to avoid. When she realized there was no escape, her desire to avoid pain subsided to make room for her desire for a potential reward. There were two reasons for this: (1) she started considering that the potential reward was worth the risk of pain, and (2) she realized that the reward was attainable, even if it was going to be hard.

Go Hard or Go Home: Avoid All-or-Nothing Thinking

There are a number of cognitive distortions that can have a negative impact on your child's vision of success. We cannot cover them all in this text, but I will address what I think to be the most important one for a fiber-less teenager. It is a distorted view of the world I like to call the "Go hard or go home" mindset. I was recently reminded of this mentality while working out at my local gym.

When you work out consistently at the same gym for a while, you begin to notice people. For me, there is one guy in particular who has, for better or for worse, left a lasting impression on my mind. Without fail, at 7:00 every morning, he comes strutting in, all 275 pounds of him, pointing and shouting at people across the gym, "Go hard or go home, baby!" I've never been able to figure out if he actually knows the people he is shouting to, but if he's trying to meet people, he should really take time to read

Dale Carnegie's book *How to Win Friends and Influence People*. If he has ever directed the challenge to me personally, I could not tell you, because when I see him coming, I avert my eyes, turn up the volume on my iPod, and start praying, "Dear God, please don't let him eat me!"

On one occasion (once my panic attack subsided), I considered his statement: "Go hard or go home." How many of us have applied this statement to our lives? Here are some examples I thought of:

- Dieting: "Oh well, I gave in and had that pizza. I might as well eat the cannoli too."
- Exercise: "I'm so tired this morning. I think I'll go to the gym tomorrow when I am feeling a little more rested."
- Work: "I'm sorry, honey, I'm not going to make it home for dinner tonight. This marketing presentation has to be perfect or else I'm going to bomb it tomorrow."
- Parenting: "I am such a failure as a parent. All the other moms are working full-time jobs while homeschooling their seven children and training for the Hawaii Ironman competition."
- Ministry: "I'm just one voice. What I say or do doesn't really matter. Anyway, the minister is the one who has been called to this. He can handle it."

I could continue the list ad infinitum, but the point is that anyone who tries to ascribe to the "go hard or go home" mind-set usually ends up going home, crawling into bed, and watching reruns of their favorite '80s television show. Why? Because no one can go hard all the time, and those who do end up burning out. "Go hard or go home" is an example of what professional therapists call all-or-nothing thinking. Some more examples:

- "If I can't be perfect, then I must be a failure."
- "If I can't be at every meeting, then I'm not going to volunteer at all."
- "If this one girl doesn't find me attractive, then I must be ugly."
- "If I don't have 5 million followers on Twitter, then what's the point of tweeting?"

This mind-set affects our actions, and it affects our view of ourselves. For example, let's say that you would like to start working out, but you don't because you're not in shape. (Consider the logic of that statement first, by the way.) Well, your goal might simply be to get to the gym every day. How intensely you work out doesn't matter at this point. You just need to get there! Accomplish that step, and then look at hopping on the treadmill the next time. If you are socially isolating yourself because you fear being rejected, consider this: if you reach out to one hundred people and 80 percent of them reject you, that still leaves twenty people who want to be your friend. Instead of looking at the eighty rejections, consider that you just went from zero to twenty.

How about your view of yourself? If you are not the star athlete, the top sales associate, the supermom or dad, the greatest (fill in the blank), that does not mean you are stupid, unsuccessful, insignificant, or a failure. Most of us are somewhere in between. Striving for excellence is a process, one that requires pacing and patience. Striving for perfection is insanity and will only make you miserable. Your fiber-less teenager struggles with the same mentality. Your job as a parent is to communicate with her that it is okay to fail in the process of change.

So the next time you see your fiber-less teenager believing the "go hard or go home" mind-set, help her consider these alternatives:

- Something is better than nothing.
- Perfection is not the goal; excellence is.
- Excellence is always achievable if you remember that it is a process that never ends, it requires patience and hard work, and it allows for our continual growth in successes and in failures, no matter where we are on the journey.
- Growth occurs in ebbs and flows. Don't get discouraged when you get tired, fail to meet expectations, or disappoint others. Remind yourself of steps 1, 2, and 3, and keep moving forward.

You must believe in your adolescent and in yourself as a parent. You both have the intelligence and the moral framework for life. Your teenager just needs the courage to function independently, and you may too. You both need courage to face failure and imperfection. You can be the impetus for that change if you are able to fight the urge to intervene and fix every problem your teenager has.

Maintain Compassion When Change Comes Slowly

Every one of us has been judged, rightly or wrongly, by another human being at some point. We've all been told that we are wrong, that we need to change, that we are headed in the wrong direction. Each of us, too, has gotten frustrated when we do not see the kind of change we had hoped for in others and in ourselves. You may be feeling a great deal of frustration with yourself and your zombie teenager at the lack of change you see in her life, despite all the changes you've been trying to implement with her. Whether she is a spark-less zombie, a pulse-less zombie, or a fiber-less zombie, you may feel like you are fighting a losing battle.

I have been practicing psychiatry for more than ten years now, and I have come to realize that the process of change is complex and difficult. For some of my clients, success and failure are measured by whether or not they can get out of bed in the morning, let alone make it to their jobs, the gym, or geometry class. There are some who know all too well what they *should* do but feel trapped by what they are *compelled* to do. Their spirits are willing. Their bodies are weak. We, as outside observers, might be quick to judge them. We theorize, often incorrectly, that they fail to change because they *will not*. They, however, would plead with us to understand that it is not a matter of willingness. They simply *cannot*. This may be the case with your teenager. In the face of these conflicting interpretations of reality, you are left with a difficult decision: Do you judge and condemn her? Do you label her? Do you shun her? Do you chalk her situation up to a lack of faith, a moral weakness, a stubbornness of pride? Or do you remain with her in the mystery of her struggle, accept your own insecurities associated with unanswerable questions, and feel the burden of her pain to whatever extent is possible?

The truth is, no one can know the depths of the human heart! We find ourselves deceived by it constantly. To judge is to say, "I know your heart!" When we get past all the rules, laws, boundaries, ultimatums, punishments, and demands in our relationships, we are still left with that not-knowing. Did they change out of fear or out of love? Did they stay the same out of fear or out of love? Who can know for sure?

I have found that those who try a cookie-cutter, one-size-fits-all, black-and-white answer for the challenges and triumphs of human growth and change do so for their own comfort and security. When they are faced with a situation or person they do not understand, these people have to force their own understanding of reality on that person or situation because they cannot deal with any unknowns. "Accept my truth, my reality, or get away from me. I can't stand you if you don't. You are a threat to me."

I must admit that, for a long time, I was that person. I was the fiber-less zombie, trying to look like I had it all together and judging others if they didn't. If I'm honest, I still struggle against that old man inside of me. We all do. Humans have an inherent need to compartmentalize truth in order to survive. When confronted with another person's experience, one that may contradict our own reality, we feel the need to pound her square peg into our round hole. We long for a clear cause-and-effect relationship to explain why she is "that way."

So-and-so relapsed on alcohol or drugs? It must mean he did not work hard enough in his recovery. Jane Doe can't seem to lose weight? It must mean she is lazy. But when you delve into the human psyche and spirit, these explanations are too cheap. If we were to ask why so-and-so didn't work hard enough or why Jane Doe lacked motivation, suddenly the picture of reality becomes fuzzy. Now we find ourselves playing with a set of psychological rabbit ears that sit atop life's static-filled TV screen. We are hoping to find a perfect position of clarity that enables us to make sense of what's playing out before us. This we do in order to avoid the fracturing of our fragile worldviews, worldviews that make no room for mystery. Herein lies the essence of all pride, prejudice, and judgment.

Very few people are capable of change in the face of such pride and spiritual prejudice. I have realized this both professionally and personally. During an extremely dark time in my own quasi-adolescence, I had people who spoke truth to me, but in two different ways. The first group demanded that I accept their understanding of the situation and conform to their rules of reality. They left no room or time for my acclamation to their truth, nor did they display any desire to understand my reality, the one in which I felt trapped at the time.

Looking back, I can honestly say I was incapable of seeing or conforming to their truth. The only way I know how to describe that pain is by likening it to a prisoner, chained to a wall, enduring the shouts of angry inquisitors, crying, "Free yourself!" all the while writhing to the point of bloodshed against the shackles and shouting back, "Don't you get it? I can't!" One man, who at an earlier time in our relationship claimed I was like a second son to him, told me in the midst of my despair, "You made your bed. Now it's time for you to sleep in it." He was correct, of course, but his admonition did nothing to help me change. A minister's wife looked at me straight in the eyes and exclaimed, "You disgust me!" She, too, was correct. I was worthy of her disgust, but there again, her words did nothing to help me but simply hardened my heart even more.

Then came salvation: another group of people who spoke truth into my life, but in an entirely different way. It is to these people I am indebted for the changes I've experienced in my heart and life over the years. They were and still are the people who have said time and time again, "I get it, I love you, I am here." There was no need for judgment or condemnation. They knew I had done enough of that to myself, and it was going to take time for me to come out of it. Instead of abandoning me, they refused to give up on me. The difference between the two groups can be summed up in one word: *compassion*!

Now, understand me: I do not condemn the people in the first group (or at least I try hard not to). I know I have been guilty of inflicting the same judgment and condemnation on others. It is not easy to love others when our own survival depends on maintaining a rigid, unbending reality that cannot tolerate the mysterious. If you are reading this and I have been the person who has judged you, or perhaps spoken truth into your life but without the necessary compassion you needed at the time, please forgive me. We all need compassion, even for our failure to show compassion.

But I would also like to challenge each of us to contemplate what is that one necessary ingredient in your relationships that must be present in order to lead to lasting change? In *The Brothers Karamazov*, Dostoyevsky sums up the answer to my question perfectly. Though long, this passage is one of the most succinct and compelling treatises on compassion I have ever read. A man stands trial for murder, and his lawyer, asking for leniency from the court, echoes what we all long for in the midst of our failures and misunderstandings:

I swear that, if you condemn him, you will only make it easier for his conscience, for he will end by cursing the man whose blood was spilled, instead of weeping for him. At the same time, you will destroy the man he could have been, because you will doom him to remain blind and embittered for the rest of his life. On the other hand, wouldn't you rather punish him sternly and painfully, indeed, inflict upon him the worst punishment imaginable, but a punishment that will save his soul and regenerate him? If so, then smother him with your mercy: Then you will see and hear him flinch and shudder in awe: "How am I to endure this mercy? What have I done to deserve so much love? Can I ever become worthy of it?" Yes, this is what his heart will cry out . . . and he will bow before your great act of mercy, because he is yearning for an act of love, and his heart will catch fire and he will be saved forever and ever![4]

As you work with your teenage zombie, set boundaries. Enforce consequences consistently. Recognize your own limitations to help her. Step back, as hard as it may be, and let her fail. But at all costs, don't condemn her or yourself. Never give up hope that she can be resurrected. As you struggle through what to do with her, you will be glad you kept your compassion and tried to relate to her, letting her struggles change you as well. May all of us pray, "God help me to grow in my compassion for people every day. Amen!"

Here is a test of the depths of your compassion for your teenager. On a scale of 1 to 5, to what extent can you repeat these statements to someone you know who is struggling?

- No matter how long it takes, I will always love you.
- No matter how long it takes, I will keep seeking to understand your struggle.
- No matter how long it takes, I will never lose faith in the process of your transformation.
- No matter how long it takes, I will never give up hope that you can see this to the end.

Strategy Questions

1. If you have a fiber-less zombie in your home, in what areas of life do you see him or her being afraid to fail?
2. How can you allow your child the opportunity to fail while still being supportive and compassionate toward his or her struggle? How might your fears and anxieties be interfering with this process, and what can you do to overcome them?

AFTERWORD

Winning the Battle for
Your Teenage Zombie

will never forget my experience with Brian, the patient I saw
early on in my career. That experience and many more like it
would convince me, once and for all, that the undead are real.
No, I don't have a bomb shelter behind my house stocked with
guns and canned goods, but hopefully this book has made us
mindful of a growing epidemic of dissatisfaction and direction-
lessness in the lives of adolescents that has begun to deaden their
hearts, minds, and spirits.

Still, there is hope! Just listen to Brian's words, now a thirty-
two-year-old software developer and former zombie, writing
to his parents after being promoted to project manager at his
company:

Dear Mom and Dad,

Thanks so much for putting up with me all these years.
I know I was a beast at times and really put you through hell,
but I appreciate that you never gave up on me. Now that I have
kids of my own, I recognize the sacrifices you made to give
me a chance in life. I will not forget that. I know that neither

of you is perfect. Far from it, right? ☺ (And, of course, I know you know I'm not either!) But you were exactly the parents I needed, even though I hated you for it at times. Laura [his wife] and I dedicate this promotion to both of you. I love you both so much.

Always your son,
Brian

If you are a parent of an undead adolescent, there is hope for you and your child. My hope is that by reading this book, you have gained insight into the nature of your child's struggles and will adopt some practical advice on how to confront your own fears, avoid being consumed, and successfully transform the undead adolescent in your home back into the son or daughter you knew and loved. But if you are going to resurrect your child, you must first accept the battle waiting for you.

The Battle for the Undead

If you long for a redemptive experience like the one Brian and his parents had, there are three important decisions you must make. First, refuse to admit defeat. There is no "game over." The credits do not roll until you draw your final breath. While people live, there is always an opportunity for a redeeming experience between them. Even those of you who have lost a child to suicide, drug overdose, or the consequences of a chronic mental illness have the opportunity to make a difference in the lives of your other children, in families who may be at risk of experiencing what you did, and in society through the power of your story and voice.

Take Rick Warren, the pastor of Saddleback Church, as an example. He wrote the now famous Purpose Driven Life series. His son committed suicide after battling bipolar disorder for many years. Despite the pain of that loss, Rick and his wife, Kay, have stayed true to the theme of their lives and striven to find purpose beyond the suffering. They now host a Mental Health Awareness Conference at their church, which has reached thousands of people.[1] If you have ever watched an apocalyptic movie, you know that devastation and destruction are always followed by rebirth and rebuilding. You cannot give up on that hope.

Second, be willing to take drastic measures. In horror flicks, the people who do not understand the severity of their circumstances are the first to be destroyed, or worse yet, become a member of the undead. This book may have challenged you to do things that seem counterintuitive for a loving, caring parent such as yourself. Your gut reaction tells you, *This will not work!* All I can say is, try as hard as possible to withhold your final judgment until you have taken time to reflect on the needs of your son or daughter and on your own predispositions as a parent. You will be testing the limits of your mental and emotional strength and endurance. Do not let your fear paralyze you from acting in a way that may be painful in the short term but will set the stage for victory in the end.

Finally, be willing to tailor the attack strategies listed in this text to fit your specific circumstances. A survival guide can give general rules to follow, but every situation is different. I am convinced that resurrecting the undead in your life is less about a formulaic, step-by-step process and more about asking the right questions to (1) understand the nature of the undead before you, and (2) understand your own nature in reacting to him or her.

The more intentional you are, the better you will handle any unpredictable scenarios that might arise in your home. No more popcorn-spilling jump scares for you. That is why I have listed the questions at the end of each chapter to help you tailor the principles you have learned to your own situation. Do not gloss over these questions. Go back and take your time with each of them. They could be a matter of life or death to you and your undead adolescent.

As a parent, you know that the path toward resurrecting a teenage zombie is a long and challenging one, but it is also one lined with great rewards for both you and your child. I do not know where you are in the journey. Some of you have children who are not yet adolescents. You are way ahead of the game, and I applaud you for preparing early for the challenges that await you. Some of you have children that are in the thick of it this very moment. May you find the spark, pulse, and fiber you need to keep moving forward. Then there are those of you who have children who are way past their adolescence but seem to have fallen prey to the deadness of a purposeless life. My prayer is that you will not lose hope in and for your son or daughter. Resurrection is always just over the horizon and redemption just around the corner. Hold out for one more day.

Finally, there is one last group that might be reading this book. You are that person who is willing to acknowledge that you've become one of the walking dead. You feel the deadness that is inside of you, and you are desperate for a cure. My prayer for you is that you will use the tools in this book not only to find life, but to thrive in it, through it, and beyond it. Now "stay calm" and start resurrecting zombies!

NOTES

CHAPTER 1: THE TEENAGE ZOMBIE DEFINED

1. E. H. Erikson (1963). *Childhood and Society*, 2nd ed. (New York: Norton, 1963).
2. American Psychiatric Association, *Diagnostic and Statistical Manual of Mental Disorders: DSM-5* (Arlington, VA: American Psychiatric Association, 2013), 160.
3. D. Olweus, A. Mattsson, D. Schalling, and H. Löw, "Testosterone, Aggression, Physical, and Personality Dimensions in Normal Adolescent Males," *Psychosomatic Medicine* 42, no. 2 (January 1, 1980): 253–69.

CHAPTER 2: THE TEENAGE ZOMBIE ORIGINS

1. Carl Jung, "The Structure of the Unconscious (1916)," *Collected Works*, vol. 7 (Princeton, NJ: Princeton University Press, 1972), 263–92.
2. J. O. Balswick and J. K. Balswick, *The Family: A Christian Perspective on the Contemporary Home* (Grand Rapids, MI: Baker Academic, 2007).
3. Charles Dickens, *Great Expectations* (Champaign, IL: Project Gutenberg, 1990), 124.

4. J. J. Arnett, *Emerging Adulthood: The Winding Road from the Late Teens Through the Twenties* (New York: Oxford University Press, 2004).

5. Alan Dunn, "Failure to Launch: Adult Children Moving Back Home," Forbes.com, June 6, 2012, http://www.forbes.com/sites/moneywisewomen/2012/06/06/failure-to-launch-adult-children-moving-back-home/#1a59df552a0c.

6. "Wealthiest Countries Statistics," Statistic Brain Research Institute, December 15, 2013, http://www.statisticbrain.com/wealthiest-countries.

7. Tim Worstall, "Astonishing Numbers: America's Poor Still Live Better Than Most of the Rest of Humanity," June 1, 2013, Forbes.com, http://www.forbes.com/sites/timworstall/2013/06/01/astonishing-numbers-americas-poor-still-live-better-than-most-of-the-rest-of-humanity/#770f31fb23c4.

8. Alan Dunn, "Failure to Launch: Adult Children Moving Back Home," June 6, 2012, Forbes.com, http://www.forbes.com/sites/moneywisewomen/2012/06/06/failure-to-launch-adult-children-moving-back-home/#2dd873c2a0cf.

9. S. Turkle, *Alone Together: Why We Expect More from Technology and Less from Each Other* (New York: Basic Books, 2011).

10. B. S. Crosier, G. D. Webster, and H. M. Dillon, "Wired to Connect: Evolutionary Psychology and Social Networks," *Review of General Psychology* 16, no. 2 (2012): 230–39, doi:10.1037/a0027919.

11. Suniya S. Luthar and Shawn J. Latendresse, "Children of the Affluent: Challenges to Well-Being," *Current Directions in Psychological Science* 14, no. 1 (February 2005): 49–53.

12. Barry Schwartz, *The Paradox of Choice: Why More Is Less* (New York: HarperCollins, 2009).

13. Bureau of Labor Statistics, U.S. Department of Labor, "Youth Labor Force Participation Rate in July 2013 Same as a Year Earlier," August 23, 2013, http://www.bls.gov/opub/ted/2013/ted_20130823.htm.

14. J. J. Arnett, *Emerging Adulthood: The Winding Road from the Late Teens Through the Twenties* (New York: Oxford University Press, 2004), 146.

15. S. Turkle, *Alone Together: Why We Expect More from Technology and Less from Each Other* (New York: Basic Books, 2011), 236.

16. J. T. Spence and C. Buckner, "Masculinity and Feminity: Defining the Undefinable," in *Gender, Power, and Communication in Human Relationships*, ed. Pamela J. Kalbfleisch and Michael J. Cody (Mahwah, NJ: Erlbaum, 1995) 106.

17. J. J. Arnett, *Emerging Adulthood: The Winding Road from the Late Teens Through the Twenties* (New York: Oxford University Press, 2004), 75.

18. C. M. Buchanan, "The Impact of Divorce on Adjustment During Adolescence," in R. D. Taylor and M. Weng, eds., *Resilience Across Contexts: Family, Work, Culture, and Community* (Mahwah, NJ: Erlbaum, 2000), 179–216.

19. E. M. Hetherington, and M. Stanley-Hagan, "Diversity among Stepfamilies," in D. H. Demo and K. R. Allen, eds., *Handbook of Family Diversity* (New York: Oxford University Press, 2000), 173–96.

20. National Institute on Drug Abuse, "Drug Facts: High School and Youth Trends," National Institutes of Health; U.S. Department of Health and Human Services, revised December 2014, http://www.drugabuse.gov/publications/drugfacts/high-school-youth-trends.

21. Kristi A. DeName, "Video Games: Are They Really a Source of Addiction?" July 21, 2013, PsychCentral.com, http://psychcentral.com/blog/archives/2013/07/21/video-games-are-they-really-a-source-of-addiction/.

22. C. M. Jacobson, and M. Gould, "The Epidemiology and Phenomenology of Non-suicidal Self-injurious Behavior among Adolescents: A Critical Review of the Literature," *Arch Suicide Res. 2007*; 11(2): 129–47.

23. Public Health Service's Office in Women's Health, Eating Disorders Information Sheet, 2000, https://www.ndsu.edu/fileadmin/counseling/Eating_Disorder_Statistics.pdf.

NOTES

24. D. Neumark-Sztainer, *I'm, Like, SO Fat!* (New York: Guilford Press, 2005), 5.
25. http://www.covenanteyes.com/pornstats/.
26. Ibid.
27. http://www.cdc.gov/violenceprevention/suicide/youth_suicide.html.
28. Ibid.
29. http://www.nimh.nih.gov/health/statistics/prevalence/any -disorder-among-children.shtml.

CHAPTER 3: THE TEENAGE ZOMBIE BRAIN

1. D. Wood, J. Bruner, and G. Ross, "The Role of Tutoring in Problem Solving," *Journal of Child Psychology and Child Psychiatry* 17 (1976): 89–100.
2. S. Löwel, and W. Singer, "Selection of Intrinsic Horizontal Connections in the Visual Cortex by Correlated Neuronal Activity," United States: American Association for the Advancement of Science 255 (1992): 209–12.
3. P. Thompson et al., "Growth Patterns in the Developing Brain Detected by Using Continuum Mechanical Tensor Maps," *Nature* 404 (2000): 190–93.
4. Proverbs 15:22.

CHAPTER 4: THE TEENAGE ZOMBIE HEART

1. Galatians 5:22–23.

CHAPTER 5: THE TEENAGE ZOMBIE SPIRIT

1. Proverbs 30:7–9, author's paraphrase.
2. R. M. Berne, *Physiology* (St. Louis: Mosby, 1998), 86, 91, 97–102.
3. Jake Schaller, "Not for Bathing: Bath Salts and the New Menace of Synthetic Drugs," *Journal of Health Care Law & Policy* 16, no. 1 (2013): 245–69.
4. See C. S. Lewis, *A Grief Observed* (San Francisco: HarperSanFrancisco, 2001).

5. J. Sommers-Flanagan, and R. Sommers-Flanagan, *Counseling and Psychotherapy Theories in Context and Practice: Skills, Strategies, and Techniques* (Hoboken, NJ: J. Wiley & Sons, 2004), 146.

CHAPTER 6: THE FEAR OF DECEPTION

1. Elizabeth Landau, "Why Zombies, Robots, Clowns Freak Us Out," CNN.com, updated September 27, 2012, http://www.cnn.com/2012/07/11/health/uncanny-valley-robots/index.html.

CHAPTER 7: THE FEAR OF ASSOCIATION

1. 2 Corinthians 7:8–9.

CHAPTER 8: THE FEAR OF EXHAUSTION

1. Colossians 3:23.

CHAPTER 9: THE FEAR OF HUMILIATION

1. Matthew 5:4.
2. Matthew 7:6, author's paraphrase.
3. Jim Gaffigan, "Jim Gaffigan—Beyond the Pale—Hot Pockets," YouTube video, 4:37, posted June 2010, https://www.youtube.com/watch?v=wmHSe_S04CU.

CHAPTER 10: THE SPARK OF LIFE: MOTIVATION

1. Proverbs 4:23, author's paraphrase.
2. Genesis 2:15.
3. Mihaly Csikszentmihályi, *Flow: The Psychology of Optimal Experience* (New York: Harper & Row, 1990).

CHAPTER 11: THE PULSE OF LIFE: DIRECTION

1. P. D. Meier, and D. L. Henderson, *Finding Purpose beyond Our Pain: Uncover the Hidden Potential in Life's Most Common Struggles* (Nashville, TN: Thomas Nelson, 2009).

2. Alcoholics Anonymous, *Twelve Steps and Twelve Traditions* (New York: Alcoholics Anonymous World Services, 1981), 107.
3. Ibid.
4. Ibid.
5. Ronald Polansky, ed., *The Cambridge Companion to Aristotle's Nicomachean Ethics* (New York: Cambridge University Press, 2014), 74.

CHAPTER 12: THE FIBER OF LIFE: DETERMINATION
1. Sarah Young, *Jesus Calling* (Nashville, TN: Thomas Nelson), October 26 reading.
2. Mark 12:31.
3. 1 John 4:18.
4. Fyodor Dostoyevsky, *The Brothers Karamazov* (New York: Farrar, Straus and Giroux, 2002).

AFTERWORD
1. Christine A. Scheller, "Can Churches Separate Mental Illness and Shame?" ChristianityToday.com, March 31, 2014, http://www.christianitytoday.com/ct/2014/march-web-only/rick-warren-saddleback-mental-health.html.

ABOUT THE AUTHOR

Dr. David Henderson is a board-certified psychiatrist, author, and speaker. He is the founder and president of Four Stones Collaborative, a mental health consulting practice in Dallas, Texas. For five years, Dr. Henderson served as the department chair of psychology and counseling at Criswell College, rebuilding its masters in counseling program and starting the undergraduate major in psychology. He also helped to develop a fully online counseling curriculum for the school. In addition, Dr. Henderson has served as an adjunct professor of psychology and counseling at Dallas Theological Seminary. He serves on the board of directors for Drug Prevention Resources, Inc., a nonprofit organization dedicated to preventing youth substance abuse. Dr. Henderson has presented nationally and internationally at conferences for the American Psychiatric Association, the American Academy of Psychiatry and the Law, The Christian Association for Psychological Studies, and the Christian Medical and Dental Association. For more information, you can visit his website at www.drdavidhenderson.com.